Bahá'í
Readings

Bahá'í
Readings

Copyright © 1984
by the National Spiritual Assembly
of the Bahá'ís of Canada

First Edition, March, 1984
Second Printing, August, 1984
Third Printing, November, 1984

Second Edition, January 1985
Third Edition, April, 1992

ISBN 0-88867-041-9

Printed in Canada

BAHÁ'Í READINGS

Selections
from the Writings of
The Báb, Bahá'u'lláh and
'Abdu'l-Bahá
for daily meditation

DAILY READING
OF THE CREATIVE WORD

Recite ye the verses of God every morning and evening. Whoso reciteth them not hath truly failed to fulfill his pledge to the Covenant of God and His Testament and whoso in this day turneth away therefrom, hath indeed turned away from God since time immemorial. Fear ye God, O concourse of My servants.

Bahá'u'lláh, Kitab-i-Aqdas

Intone, O My servant, the verses of God that have been received by thee, as intoned by them who have drawn nigh unto Him, that the sweetness of thy melody may kindle thine own soul, and attract the hearts of all men. Whoso reciteth, in the privacy of his chamber, the verses revealed by God, the scattering angels of the Almighty shall scatter abroad the fragrance of the words uttered by his mouth, and shall cause the heart of every righteous man to throb. Though he may, at first, remain unaware of its effect, yet the virtue of the grace vouchsafed unto him must needs sooner or later exercise its influence upon his soul. Thus have the mysteries of the Revelation of God been decreed by virtue of the Will of Him Who is the Source of power and wisdom.   Bahá'u'lláh, *Gleanings from the Writings of Bahá'u'lláh*, pp. 294

March 21

FEAST OF GLORY

O SON OF SPIRIT!

My first counsel is this: Possess a pure, kindly and radiant heart, that thine may be a sovereignty ancient, imperishable and everlasting.

Bahá'u'lláh, *The Hidden Words of Bahá'u'lláh*, No. 1 (Arabic)

Do ye know in what cycle ye are created and in what age ye exist? This is the age of the Blessed Perfection and this is the time of the Greatest Name! This is the century of the Manifestation, the age of the Sun of the Horizons and the beautiful springtime of His Holiness the Eternal One!

The earth is in motion and growth; the mountains, hills and prairies are green and pleasant; the bounty is overflowing; the mercy universal; the rain is descending from the cloud of mercy; the brilliant Sun is shining; the full moon is ornamenting the horizon of ether; the great ocean-tide is flooding every little stream; the gifts are successive; the favours consecutive; and the refreshing breeze is blowing, wafting the fragrant perfume of the blossoms. Boundless treasure is in the hand of the King of Kings! Lift the hem of thy garment in order to receive it.

If we are not happy and joyous at this season, for what other season shall we wait and for what other time shall we look?

'Abdu'l-Bahá, *Bahá'í World Faith*, p. 351

March 22

Verily I say, this is the Day in which mankind can behold the Face, and hear the Voice, of the Promised One. The Call of God hath been raised, and the light of His countenance hath been lifted up upon men. It behoveth every man to blot out the trace of every idle word from the tablet of his heart, and to gaze, with an open and unbiased mind, on the signs of His Revelation, the proofs of His Mission, and the tokens of His glory. . . .

O thou that hast remembered Me! The most grievous veil hath shut out the peoples of the earth from His glory, and hindered them from hearkening to His call. God grant that the light of unity may envelop the whole earth, and that the seal, "the Kingdom is God's", may be stamped upon the brow of all its peoples. Bahá'u'lláh, *Gleanings from the Writings of Bahá'u'lláh*, pp. 10-11

March 23

God is My witness, O people! I was asleep on My couch, when lo, the Breeze of God wafting over Me roused Me from My slumber. His quickening Spirit revived Me, and My tongue was unloosed to voice His Call. . . . Think ye, O people, that I hold within My grasp the control of God's ultimate Will and Purpose? Far be it from Me to advance such claim. . . . Had the ultimate destiny of God's Faith been in Mine hands, I would have never consented, even though for one moment, to manifest Myself unto you, nor would I have allowed one word to fall from My lips. Of this God Himself is, verily, a witness.

Bahá'u'lláh, *Gleanings from the Writings of Bahá'u'lláh, pp. 90-91*

March 24

He Who is your Lord, the All-Merciful, cherisheth in His heart the desire of beholding the entire human race as one soul and one body. Haste ye to win your share of God's good grace and mercy in this Day that eclipseth all other created Days. How great the felicity that awaiteth the man that forsaketh all he hath in a desire to obtain the things of God! Such a man, We testify, is among God's blessed ones.

Bahá'u'lláh, *Gleanings from the Writings of Bahá'u'lláh*, p. 214

March 25

The purpose of justice is the appearance of unity among men. The ocean of divine wisdom surgeth within this exalted word, while the books of the world cannot contain its inner significance. Were mankind to be adorned with this raiment, they would behold the day-star of the utterance, "On that day God will satisfy everyone out of His abundance," shining resplendent above the horizon of the world.   Bahá'u'lláh, *Tablets of Bahá'u'lláh*, pp. 66-67

March 26

In every Dispensation the light of Divine Guidance has been focussed upon one central theme. . . . In this wondrous Revelation, this glorious century, the foundation of the Faith of God and the distinguishing feature of His Law is the consciousness of the Oneness of Mankind.

'Abdu'l-Bahá, *The World Order of Bahá'u'lláh*, p. 36

March 27

"O ye children of men, the fundamental purpose animating the Faith of God and His Religion is to safeguard the interests and promote the unity of the human race . . . This is the straight path, the fixed and immovable foundation. Whatsoever is raised on this foundation, the changes and chances of the world can never impair its strength, nor will the revolution of countless centuries undermine its structure." "The well-being of mankind, its peace and security are unattainable unless and until its unity is firmly established." "So powerful is the light of unity, that it can illuminate the whole earth. The one true God, He Who knoweth all things, Himself testifieth to the truth of these words . . . This goal excelleth every other goal, and this aspiration is the monarch of all aspirations."

Bahá'u'lláh, *The World Order of Bahá'u'lláh*, pp. 202-203

March 28

This is the Day in which God's most excellent favours have been poured out upon men, the Day in which His most mighty grace hath been infused into all created things. It is incumbent upon all the peoples of the world to reconcile their differences, and, with perfect unity and peace, abide beneath the shadow of the Tree of His care and loving-kindness. . . .

Beseech ye the one true God to grant that all men may be graciously assisted to fulfil that which is acceptable in Our sight. Soon will the present-day order be rolled up, and a new one spread out in its stead. Verily, thy Lord speaketh the truth, and is the Knower of things unseen.

Bahá'u'lláh, *Gleanings from the Writings of Bahá'u'lláh*, p. 6

March 29

"Let your principal concern be to rescue the fallen from the slough of impending extinction, and to help him embrace the ancient Faith of God. Your behaviour towards your neighbour should be such as to manifest clearly the signs of the one true God, for ye are the first among men to be re-created by His Spirit, the first to adore and bow the knee before Him, the first to circle round His throne of glory." ". . . Unloose your tongues, and proclaim unceasingly His Cause. This shall be better for you than all the treasures of the past and of the future, if ye be of them that comprehend this truth." . . . "Vie ye with each other in the service of God and of His Cause. This is indeed what profiteth you in this world, and in that which is to come. Your Lord, the God of Mercy, is the All-Informed, the All-Knowing." Bahá'u'lláh, *The Advent of Divine Justice*, p. 70

March 30

"It is not for him to pride himself who loveth his own country, but rather for him who loveth the whole world. The earth is but one country, and mankind its citizens." "That one indeed is a man who today dedicateth himself to the service of the entire human race." "Through the power released by these exalted words, He hath lent a fresh impulse, and set a new direction, to the birds of men's hearts, and hath obliterated every trace of restriction and limitation from God's Holy Book."

Bahá'u'lláh, *The World Order of Bahá'u'lláh*, p. 198

March 31

Beware lest ye contend with any one, nay, strive to make him aware of the truth with kindly manner and most convincing exhortation. If your hearer respond, he will have responded to his own behoof, and if not, turn ye away from him, and set your faces towards God's sacred Court, the seat of resplendent holiness.

Dispute not with any one concerning the things of this world and its affairs, for God hath abandoned them to such as have set their affection upon them. Out of the whole world He hath chosen for Himself the hearts of men—hearts which the hosts of revelation and of utterance can subdue.

Bahá'u'lláh, *Gleanings from the Writings of Bahá'u'lláh*, p. 279

April 1

Pollute not your tongues by speaking evil of another. Recognize your enemies as friends, and consider those who wish you evil as the wishers of good. You must not see evil as evil and then compromise with your opinion, for to treat in a smooth, kindly way one whom you consider evil or an enemy is hypocrisy, and this is not worthy or allowable. You must consider your enemies as your friends, look upon your evil-wishers as your well-wishers and treat them accordingly. Act in such a way that your heart may be free from hatred. Let not your heart be offended with anyone. If some one commits an error and wrong toward you, you must instantly forgive him. Do not complain of others. Refrain from reprimanding them, and if you wish to give admonition or advice, let it be offered in such a way that it will not burden the hearer. Turn all your thoughts toward bringing joy to hearts.

Abdu'l-Bahá, *Promulgation of Universal Peace*,
(1982 edition), p. 453

April 2

The true seeker hunteth naught but the object of his quest, and the lover hath no desire save union with his beloved. Nor shall the seeker reach his goal unless he sacrifice all things. That is, whatever he hath seen, and heard, and understood, all must he set at naught, that he may enter the realm of the spirit, which is the City of God. Labour is needed, if we are to seek Him; ardour is needed, if we are to drink of the honey of reunion with Him; and if we taste of this cup, we shall cast away the world.

Bahá'u'lláh, *The Seven Valleys and the Four Valleys*, p. 7

April 3

Worship thou God in such wise that if thy worship lead thee to the fire, no alteration in thine adoration would be produced, and so likewise if thy recompense should be paradise. Thus and thus alone should be the worship which befitteth the one True God. Shouldst thou worship Him because of fear, this would be unseemly in the sanctified Court of His presence, and could not be regarded as an act by thee dedicated to the Oneness of His Being. Or if thy gaze should be on paradise, and thou shouldst worship Him while cherishing such a hope, thou wouldst make God's creation a partner with Him, notwithstanding the fact that paradise is desired by men.

Fire and paradise both bow down and prostrate themselves before God. That which is worthy of His Essence is to worship Him for His sake, without fear of fire, or hope of paradise.

The Báb, *Selections from the Writings of the Báb*, pp. 77-78

April 4

The most acceptable prayer is the one offered with the utmost spirituality and radiance; its prolongation hath not been and is not beloved by God. The more detached and the purer the prayer, the more acceptable is it in the presence of God.

The Báb, *Selections from the Writings of the Báb*, p. 78

April 5

The obligatory prayers are binding inasmuch as they are conducive to humility and submissiveness, to setting one's face toward God and expressing devotion to Him. Through such prayer man holdeth communion with God, seeketh to draw near unto Him, converseth with the true Beloved of one's heart, and attaineth spiritual stations.

Know thou that in every word and movement of the obligatory prayer there are allusions, mysteries and a wisdom that man is unable to comprehend, and letters and scrolls cannot contain.

'Abdu'l-Bahá, *Spiritual Foundations: Prayer, Meditation and the Devotional Attitude*, pp. 8, 9

April 6

It is seemly that the servant should, after each prayer, supplicate God to bestow mercy and forgiveness upon his parents. Thereupon God's call will be raised: "Thousand upon thousand of what thou hast asked for thy parents shall be thy recompense!" Blessed is he who remembereth his parents when communing with God. There is, verily, no God but Him, the Mighty, the Well-Beloved.

The Báb, *Selections from the Writings of the Báb*, p. 94

April 7

When the sinner findeth himself wholly detached and freed from all save God, he should beg forgiveness and pardon from Him. Confession of sins and transgressions before human beings is not permissible, as it hath never been nor will ever be conducive to divine forgiveness. Moreover such confession before people results in one's humiliation and abasement, and God—exalted be His glory—wisheth not the humiliation of His servants. Verily He is the Compassionate, the Merciful.

Bahá'u'lláh, *Tablets of Bahá'u'lláh*, p. 24

April 8

FEAST OF GLORY

The Feast hath been enjoined upon you once in every month, though it be with water only. God hath verily purposed to bring the hearts of men together, though it require every means on earth and in the heavens.

Bahá'u'lláh, *Bahá'í Meetings; The Nineteen Day Feast*, p. 17

Each one of you must think how to make happy and pleased the other members of your Assembly, and each one must consider all those who are present as better and greater than himself, and each one must consider himself less than the rest. Know their station as high, and think of your own station as low.

'Abdu'l-Bahá, *Bahá'í Meetings; The Nineteen Day Feast*, pp. 20

THE MONTH OF GLORY
BEGINS AT SUNSET

April 9

O SON OF SPIRIT!
With the joyful tidings of light I hail thee:
rejoice! To the court of holiness I summon thee;
abide therein that thou mayest live in peace for
evermore.

Bahá'u'lláh, *The Hidden Words
of Bahá'u'lláh*, No. 33 (Arabic)

April 10

The moment this Divine Message is carried forward by the American believers from the shores of America and is propagated through the continents of Europe, of Asia, of Africa and of Australasia, and as far as the islands of the Pacific, this community will find itself securely established upon the throne of an everlasting dominion. Then will all the peoples of the world witness that this community is spiritually illumined and divinely guided. Then will the whole earth resound with the praises of its majesty and greatness. . . .

O that I could travel, even though on foot and in the utmost poverty, to these regions, and, raising the call of "Yá Bahá'u'l-Abhá" in cities, villages, mountains, deserts and oceans, promote the Divine teachings! This, alas, I cannot do. How intensely I deplore it! Please God, ye may achieve it.

'Abdu'l-Bahá, *Tablets of the Divine Plan*, pp. 38-39

April 11

As regards the teachers, they must completely divest themselves from the old garments and be invested with a new garment. According to the statement of Christ, they must attain to the station of rebirth—that is, whereas in the first instance they were born from the womb of the mother, this time they must be born from the womb of the world of nature. Just as they are now totally unaware of the experiences of the fetal world, they must also forget entirely the defects of the world of nature. They must be baptized with the water of life, the fire of the love of God and the breaths of the Holy Spirit; be satisfied with little food, but take a large portion from the heavenly table.

'Abdu'l-Bahá, *Tablets of the Divine Plan*, pp. 87-88

April 12

Thou hast asked Me concerning the nature of the soul. Know, verily, that the soul is a sign of God, a heavenly gem whose reality the most learned of men hath failed to grasp, and whose mystery no mind, however acute, can ever hope to unravel. It is the first among all created things to declare the excellence of its Creator, the first to recognize His glory, to cleave to His truth, and to bow down in adoration before Him. If it be faithful to God, it will reflect His light, and will, eventually, return unto Him. If it fail, however, in its allegiance to its Creator, it will become a victim to self and passion, and will, in the end, sink in their depths.

Bahá'u'lláh, *Gleanings from the Writings of Bahá'u'lláh*, pp. 158-159

April 13

Know thou, of a truth, that if the soul of man hath walked in the ways of God, it will, assuredly, return and be gathered to the glory of the Beloved. By the righteousness of God! It shall attain a station such as no pen can depict, or tongue describe. The soul that hath remained faithful to the Cause of God, and stood unwaveringly firm in His Path shall, after his ascension, be possessed of such power that all the worlds which the Almighty hath created can benefit through him. Such a soul provideth, at the bidding of the Ideal King and Divine Educator, the pure leaven that leaveneth the world of being, and furnisheth the power through which the arts and wonders of the world are made manifest. Consider how meal needeth leaven to be leavened with. Those souls that are the symbols of detachment are the leaven of the world. Meditate on this, and be of the thankful.

Bahá'u'lláh, *Gleanings from the Writings of Bahá'u'lláh*, p. 161

April 14

When the human soul soareth out of this transient heap of dust and riseth into the world of God, then veils will fall away, and verities will come to light, and all things unknown before will be made clear, and hidden truths be understood.

Consider how a being, in the world of the womb, was deaf of ear and blind of eye, and mute of tongue; how he was bereft of any perceptions at all. But once, out of that world of darkness, he passed into this world of light, then his eye saw, his ear heard, his tongue spoke. In the same way, once he hath hastened away from this mortal place into the Kingdom of God, then he will be born in the spirit; then the eye of his perception will open, the ear of his soul will hearken, and all the truths of which he was ignorant before will be made plain and clear.

'Abdu'l-Bahá, *Selections from the Writings of 'Abdu'l-Bahá*, p. 177

April 15

The rewards of the other world are peace, the spiritual graces, the various spiritual gifts in the Kingdom of God, the gaining of the desires of the heart and the soul, and the meeting of God in the world of eternity. In the same way the punishments of the other world—that is to say, the torments of the other world—consist in being deprived of the special divine blessings and the absolute bounties, and falling into the lowest degrees of existence. He who is deprived of these divine favours, although he continues after death, is considered as dead by the people of truth. 'Abdu'l-Bahá, *Some Answered Questions*, (1982 edition) pp. 224-225

April 16

Whoso hath, in this Day, refused to allow the doubts and fancies of men to turn him away from Him Who is the Eternal Truth, and hath not suffered the tumult provoked by the ecclesiastical and secular authorities to deter him from recognizing His Message, such a man will be regarded by God, the Lord of all men, as one of His mighty signs, and will be numbered among them whose names have been inscribed by the Pen of the Most High in His Book. Blessed is he that hath recognized the true stature of such a soul, that hath acknowledged its station, and discovered its virtues.

Bahá'u'lláh, *Gleanings from the Writings of Bahá'u'lláh*, p. 159

April 17

Be generous in prosperity, and thankful in adversity. Be worthy of the trust of thy neighbour, and look upon him with a bright and friendly face. Be a treasure to the poor, an admonisher to the rich, an answerer of the cry of the needy, a preserver of the sanctity of thy pledge. Be fair in thy judgment, and guarded in thy speech. Be unjust to no man, and show all meekness to all men. Be as a lamp unto them that walk in darkness, a joy to the sorrowful, a sea for the thirsty, a haven for the distressed, an upholder and defender of the victim of oppression. Let integrity and uprightness distinguish all thine acts. Be a home for the stranger, a balm to the suffering, a tower of strength for the fugitive. Be eyes to the blind, and a guiding light unto the feet of the erring. Be an ornament to the countenance of truth, a crown to the brow of fidelity, a pillar of the temple of righteousness, a breath of life to the body of mankind, an ensign of the hosts of justice, a luminary above the horizon of virtue, a dew to the soil of the human heart, an ark on the ocean of knowledge, a sun in the heaven of bounty, a gem on the diadem of wisdom, a shining light in the firmament of thy generation, a fruit upon the tree of humility. Bahá'u'lláh, *Gleanings from the Writings of Bahá'u'lláh*, p. 285

April 18

Man must consult on all matters, whether major or minor, so that he may become cognizant of what is good. Consultation giveth him insight into things and enableth him to delve into questions which are unknown. The light of truth shineth from the faces of those who engage in consultation. Such consultation causeth the living waters to flow in the meadows of man's reality, the rays of ancient glory to shine upon him, and the tree of his being to be adorned with wondrous fruit. The members who are consulting, however, should behave in the utmost love, harmony and sincerity towards each other. The principle of consultation is one of the most fundamental elements of the divine edifice. Even in their ordinary affairs the individual members of society should consult.

'Abdu'l-Bahá, *Consultation: A Compilation*, p. 8

April 19

The members thereof (i.e. of a Spiritual Assembly) must take counsel together in such wise that no occasion for ill-feeling or discord may arise. This can be attained when every member expresseth with absolute freedom his own opinion and setteth forth his argument. Should anyone oppose, he must on no account feel hurt for not until matters are fully discussed can the right way be revealed. The shining spark of truth cometh forth only after the clash of differing opinions. If after discussion, a decision be carried unanimously well and good; but if, the Lord forbid, differences of opinion should arise, a majority of voices must prevail.

'Abdu'l-Bahá, *Selections from the Writings of 'Abdu'l-Bahá*, p. 87

April 20

. . . found ye Spiritual Assemblies, for these are the basis for spreading the sweet savours of God, exalting His Word, uplifting the lamp of His grace, promulgating His religion and promoting His Teachings, and what bounty is there greater than this? These Spiritual Assemblies are aided by the Spirit of God. Their defender is 'Abdu'l-Bahá. Over them He spreadeth His wings. What bounty is there greater than this? These Spiritual Assemblies are shining lamps and heavenly gardens, from which the fragrances of holiness are diffused over all regions, and the lights of knowledge are shed abroad over all created things. From them the spirit of life streameth in every direction. They, indeed, are the potent sources of the progress of man, at all times and under all conditions. What bounty is there greater than this?

'Abdu'l-Bahá, *Selections from the Writings of 'Abdu'l-Bahá*, p. 80

THE FESTIVAL OF RIDVÁN (APRIL 21 – MAY 2) BEGINS AT SUNSET. THE FIRST DAY OF RIDVÁN SHOULD BE OBSERVED AT ABOUT 3:00 P.M., APRIL 21

April 21

Consider the hour at which the supreme Manifestation of God revealeth Himself unto men. Ere that hour cometh, the Ancient Being, Who is still unknown of men and hath not as yet given utterance to the Word of God, is Himself the All-Knower in a world devoid of any man that hath known Him. He is indeed the Creator without a creation. For at the very moment preceding His Revelation, each and every created thing shall be made to yield up its soul to God. This is indeed the Day of which it hath been written: "Whose shall be the Kingdom this Day?" And none can be found ready to answer! Bahá'u'lláh, *Gleanings from the Writings of Bahá'u'lláh*, p. 151

April 22

Say: This is the Paradise on whose foliage the wine of utterance hath imprinted the testimony: "He that was hidden from the eyes of men is revealed, girded with sovereignty and power!" This is the Paradise, the rustling of whose leaves proclaims: "O ye that inhabit the heavens and the earth! There hath appeared what hath never previously appeared. He Who, from everlasting, had concealed His Face from the sight of creation is now come." From the whispering breeze that wafteth amidst its branches there cometh the cry: "He Who is the sovereign Lord of all is made manifest. The Kingdom is God's," while from its streaming waters can be heard the murmur: "All eyes are gladdened, for He Whom none hath beheld, Whose secret no one hath discovered, hath lifted the veil of glory, and uncovered the countenance of Beauty."

Bahá'u'lláh, *Gleanings from the Writings of Bahá'u'lláh*, p. 31

April 23

This is the Day whereon the Ocean of God's mercy hath been manifested unto men, the Day in which the Day Star of His loving-kindness hath shed its radiance upon them, the Day in which the clouds of His bountiful favour have overshadowed the whole of mankind. Now is the time to cheer and refresh the down-cast through the invigorating breeze of love and fellowship, and the living waters of friendliness and charity. . . .

The whole duty of man in this Day is to attain that share of the flood of grace which God poureth forth for him. Let none, therefore, consider the largeness or smallness of the receptacle. The portion of some might lie in the palm of a man's hand, the portion of others might fill a cup, and of others even a gallon-measure.

Bahá'u'lláh, *Gleanings from the Writings of Bahá'u'lláh*, pp. 7-8

38

April 24

The first duty prescribed by God for His servants is the recognition of Him Who is the Day Spring of His Revelation and the Fountain of His laws, Who representeth the Godhead in both the Kingdom of His Cause and the world of creation. Whoso achieveth this duty hath attained unto all good; and whoso is deprived thereof, hath gone astray, though he be the author of every righteous deed. It behoveth every one who reacheth this most sublime station, this summit of transcendent glory, to observe every ordinance of Him Who is the Desire of the world. These twin duties are inseparable. Neither is acceptable without the other. Thus hath it been decreed by Him Who is the Source of Divine inspiration.

Bahá'u'lláh, *Gleanings from the Writings of Bahá'u'lláh*, pp. 330-331

April 25

The world is in travail, and its agitation waxeth day by day. Its face is turned towards waywardness and unbelief. Such shall be its plight, that to disclose it now would not be meet and seemly. Its perversity will long continue. And when the appointed hour is come, there shall suddenly appear that which shall cause the limbs of mankind to quake. Then, and only then, will the Divine Standard be unfurled, and the Nightingale of Paradise warble its melody.

Bahá'u'lláh, *Gleanings from the Writings of Bahá'u'lláh*, pp. 118-119

April 26

We can well perceive how the whole human race is encompassed with great, with incalculable afflictions. We see it languishing on its bed of sickness, sore-tried and disillusioned. They that are intoxicated by self-conceit have interposed themselves between it and the Divine and infallible Physician. Witness how they have entangled all men, themselves included, in the mesh of their devices. They can neither discover the cause of the disease, nor have they any knowledge of the remedy. They have conceived the straight to be crooked, and have imagined their friend an enemy.

Incline your ears to the sweet melody of this Prisoner. Arise, and lift up your voices, that haply they that are fast asleep may be awakened. Say: O ye who are as dead! The Hand of Divine bounty proffereth unto you the Water of Life. Hasten and drink your fill. Whoso hath been re-born in this Day, shall never die; whoso remaineth dead, shall never live.

Bahá'u'lláh, *Gleanings from the Writings of Bahá'u'lláh*, p. 213

April 27

FEAST OF BEAUTY

The Nineteen Day Feast was inaugurated by the Báb and ratified by Bahá'u'lláh, in His holy book, the *Aqdas*, so that people may gather together and outwardly show fellowship and love, that the divine mysteries may be disclosed. The object is concord, that through this fellowship hearts may become perfectly united, and reciprocity and mutual helpfulness be established. Because the members of the world of humanity are unable to exist without being banded together, cooperation and mutual helpfulness is the basis of human society. Without the realization of these two great principles no great movement is pressed forward.

'Abdu'l-Bahá, *Bahá'í Meetings;*
The Nineteen Day Feast, p. 21

THE MONTH OF BEAUTY
BEGINS AT SUNSET

April 28

O SON OF BEING!
    Love Me, that I may love thee. If thou lovest Me not, My love can in no wise reach thee. Know this, O servant.
Bahá'u'lláh, The Hidden Words of Bahá'u'lláh, No. 5 (Arabic)

April 29

Call out to Zion, O Carmel, and announce the joyful tidings: He that was hidden from mortal eyes is come! His all-conquering sovereignty is manifest; His all-encompassing splendour is revealed. Beware lest thou hesitate or halt. Hasten forth and circumambulate the City of God that hath descended from heaven, the celestial Kaaba round which have circled in adoration the favoured of God, the pure in heart, and the company of the most exalted angels. Oh, how I long to announce unto every spot on the surface of the earth, and to carry to each one of its cities, the glad-tidings of this Revelation—a Revelation to which the heart of Sinai hath been attracted, and in whose name the Burning Bush is calling:

"Unto God, the Lord of Lords, belong the kingdoms of earth and heaven." Verily this is the Day in which both land and sea rejoice at this announcement, the Day for which have been laid up those things which God, through a bounty beyond the ken of mortal mind or heart, hath destined for revelation. Ere long will God sail His Ark upon thee, and will manifest the people of Baha who have been mentioned in the Book of Names. Bahá'u'lláh, *Gleanings from the Writings of Bahá'u'lláh*, p. 16

April 30

The world's equilibrium hath been upset through the vibrating influence of this most great, this new World Order. Mankind's ordered life hath been revolutionized through the agency of this unique, this wondrous System—the like of which mortal eyes have never witnessed.

Immerse yourselves in the ocean of My words, that ye may unravel its secrets, and discover all the pearls of wisdom that lie hid in its depths. Take heed that ye do not vacillate in your determination to embrace the truth of this Cause—a Cause through which the potentialities of the might of God have been revealed, and His sovereignty established. With faces beaming with joy, hasten ye unto Him. This is the changeless Faith of God, eternal in the past, eternal in the future. Let him that seeketh, attain it; and as to him that hath refused to seek it—verily, God is Self-Sufficient.

Bahá'u'lláh, *Synopsis and Codification of the Kitab-i-Aqdas*, pp. 27-28

May 1

The men of God's House of Justice have been charged with the affairs of the people. They, in truth, are the Trustees of God among His servants and the daysprings of authority in His countries.

O people of God! That which traineth the world is Justice, for it is upheld by two pillars, reward and punishment. These two pillars are the sources of life to the world. Inasmuch as for each day there is a new problem and for every problem an expedient solution, such affairs should be referred to the Ministers of the House of Justice that they may act according to the needs and requirements of the time. They that, for the sake of God, arise to serve His Cause, are the recipients of divine inspiration from the unseen Kingdom. It is incumbent upon all to be obedient unto them. Bahá'u'lláh, *Tablets of Bahá'u'lláh*, pp. 26-27

May 2

"This Day a door is open wider than both heaven and earth. The eye of the mercy of Him Who is the Desire of the worlds is turned towards all men. An act, however infinitesimal, is, when viewed in the mirror of the knowledge of God, mightier than a mountain. Every drop proffered in His path is as the sea in that mirror. For this is the Day which the one true God, glorified be He, hath announced in all His Books unto His Prophets and His Messengers." "This is a Revelation, under which, if a man shed for its sake one drop of blood, myriads of oceans will be his recompense."

Bahá'u'lláh, *The Advent of Divine Justice*, pp. 65-66

May 3

All-praise to the unity of God, and all-honour to Him, the sovereign Lord, the incomparable and all-glorious Ruler of the universe, Who, out of utter nothingness, hath created the reality of all things, Who, from naught, hath brought into being the most refined and subtle elements of His creation, and Who, rescuing His creatures from the abasement of remoteness and the perils of ultimate extinction, hath received them into His kingdom of incorruptible glory. Nothing short of His all-encompassing grace, His all-pervading mercy, could have possibly achieved it. How could it, otherwise, have been possible for sheer nothingness to have acquired by itself the worthiness and capacity to emerge from its state of non-existence into the realm of being?

Bahá'u'lláh, *Gleanings from the Writings of Bahá'u'lláh*, pp. 64-65

May 4

Having created the world and all that liveth and moveth therein, He, through the direct operation of His unconstrained and sovereign Will, chose to confer upon man the unique distinction and capacity to know Him and to love Him—a capacity that must needs be regarded as the generating impulse and the primary purpose underlying the whole of creation. . . . Upon the inmost reality of each and every created thing He hath shed the light of one of His names, and made it a recipient of the glory of one of His attributes. Upon the reality of man, however, He hath focused the radiance of all of His names and attributes, and made it a mirror of His own Self. Alone of all created things man hath been singled out for so great a favour, so enduring a bounty.

Bahá'u'lláh, *Gleanings from the Writings*
of Bahá'u'lláh, p. 65

May 5

These energies with which the Day Star of Divine bounty and Source of heavenly guidance hath endowed the reality of man lie, however, latent within him, even as the flame is hidden within the candle and the rays of light are potentially present in the lamp. The radiance of these energies may be obscured by worldly desires even as the light of the sun can be concealed beneath the dust and dross which cover the mirror. Neither the candle nor the lamp can be lighted through their own unaided efforts, nor can it ever be possible for the mirror to free itself from its dross. It is clear and evident that until a fire is kindled the lamp will never be ignited, and unless the dross is blotted out from the face of the mirror it can never represent the image of the sun nor reflect its light and glory.

Bahá'u'lláh, *Gleanings from the Writings of Bahá'u'lláh*, pp. 65-66

May 6

And since there can be no tie of direct intercourse to bind the one true God with His creation, and no resemblance whatever can exist between the transient and the Eternal, the contingent and the Absolute, He hath ordained that in every age and dispensation a pure and stainless Soul be made manifest in the kingdoms of earth and heaven. Unto this subtle, this mysterious and ethereal Being He hath assigned a twofold nature; the physical, pertaining to the world of matter, and the spiritual, which is born of the substance of God Himself. He hath, moreover, conferred upon Him a double station. The first station, which is related to His innermost reality, representeth Him as One Whose voice is the voice of God Himself. . . . The second station is the human station, . . . These Essences of Detachment, these resplendent Realities are the channels of God's all-pervasive grace. Led by the light of unfailing guidance, and invested with supreme sovereignty, They are commissioned to use the inspiration of Their words, the effusions of Their infallible grace and the sanctifying breeze of Their Revelation for the cleansing of every longing heart and receptive spirit from the dross and dust of earthly cares and limitations. Then, and only then, will the Trust of God, latent in the reality of man, emerge, as resplendent as the rising Orb of Divine Revelation, from behind the veil of concealment, and implant the ensign of its revealed glory upon the summits of men's hearts.

Bahá'u'lláh, *Gleanings from the Writings of Bahá'u'lláh*, pp. 66-67

May 7

From the foregoing passages and allusions it hath been made indubitably clear that in the kingdoms of earth and heaven there must needs be manifested a Being, an Essence Who shall act as a Manifestation and Vehicle for the transmission of the grace of the Divinity Itself, the Sovereign Lord of all. Through the Teachings of this Day Star of Truth every man will advance and develop until he attaineth the station at which he can manifest all the potential forces with which his inmost true self hath been endowed. It is for this very purpose that in every age and dispensation the Prophets of God and His chosen Ones have appeared amongst men, and have evinced such power as is born of God and such might as only the Eternal can reveal.

Bahá'u'lláh, *Gleanings from the Writings
of Bahá'u'lláh*, pp. 67-68

May 8

Beware, O believers in the Unity of God, lest ye be tempted to make any distinction between any of the Manifestations of His Cause, or to discriminate against the signs that have accompanied and proclaimed their Revelation. This indeed is the true meaning of Divine Unity, if ye be of them that apprehend and believe this truth. Be ye assured, moreover, that the works and acts of each and every one of these Manifestations of God, nay whatever pertaineth unto them, and whatsoever they may manifest in the future, are all ordained by God, and are a reflection of His Will and Purpose. Whoso maketh the slightest possible difference between their persons, their words, their messages, their acts and manners, hath indeed disbelieved in God, hath repudiated His signs, and betrayed the Cause of His Messengers.   Bahá'u'lláh, *Gleanings from the Writings of Bahá'u'lláh*, pp. 59-60

May 9

Know of a certainty that in every Dispensation the light of Divine Revelation hath been vouchsafed to men in direct proportion to their spiritual capacity. Consider the sun. How feeble its rays the moment it appeareth above the horizon. How gradually its warmth and potency increase as it approacheth its zenith, enabling meanwhile all created things to adapt themselves to the growing intensity of its light. . . . In like manner, if the Sun of Truth were suddenly to reveal, at the earliest stages of its manifestation, the full measure of the potencies which the providence of the Almighty hath bestowed upon it, the earth of human understanding would waste away and be consumed; for men's hearts would neither sustain the intensity of its revelation, nor be able to mirror forth the radiance of its light. Dismayed and overpowered, they would cease to exist.

Bahá'u'lláh, *Synopsis and Codification of the Kitáb-i-Aqdas*, p. 5

May 10

All created things have their degree or stage of maturity. The period of maturity in the life of a tree is the time of its fruit-bearing. . . . and in the human kingdom man reaches his maturity when the light of his intelligence attains its greatest power and development . . . Similarly there are periods and stages in the collective life of humanity. At one time it was passing through its stage of childhood, at another its period of youth, but now it has entered its long-predicted phase of maturity, the evidences of which are everywhere apparent . . . Man must now become imbued with new virtues and powers, new moral standards, new capacities. New bounties, perfect bestowals, are awaiting and already descending upon him. The gifts and blessings of the period of youth, although timely and sufficient during the adolescence of mankind, are now incapable of meeting the requirements of its maturity.

'Abdu'l-Bahá, *The World Order of Bahá'u'lláh*, pp. 164-165

May 11

God hath sent down His Messengers to succeed
to Moses and Jesus, and He will continue to do so till
"the end that hath no end"; so that His grace may,
from the heaven of Divine bounty, be continually
vouchsafed to mankind.

Bahá'u'lláh, *The World Order of Bahá'u'lláh*, p. 115

Concerning the Manifestations that will come
down in the future "in the shadows of the clouds,"
know verily that in so far as their relation to the
source of their inspiration is concerned they are
under the shadow of the Ancient Beauty. In their
relation, however, to the age in which they appear,
each and every one of them "doeth whatsoever He
willeth."

'Abdu'l-Bahá, *The World Order of Bahá'u'lláh*, p. 111

May 12

The essence of belief in Divine unity consisteth in regarding Him Who is the Manifestation of God and Him Who is the invisible, the inaccessible, the unknowable Essence as one and the same. By this is meant that whatever pertaineth to the former, all His acts and doings, whatever He ordaineth or forbiddeth, should be considered, in all their aspects, and under all circumstances, and without any reservation, as identical with the Will of God Himself. This is the loftiest station to which a true believer in the unity of God can ever hope to attain. Blessed is the man that reacheth this station, and is of them that are steadfast in their belief.

Bahá'u'lláh, *Gleanings from the Writings
of Bahá'u'lláh*, p. 167

May 13

Say: From My laws the sweet smelling savour of My garment can be smelled, and by their aid the standards of Victory will be planted upon the highest peaks. The Tongue of My power hath, from the heaven of My omnipotent glory, addressed to My creation these words: "Observe My commandments, for the love of My beauty." . . . By My life! He who hath drunk the choice wine of fairness from the hands of My bountiful favour, will circle around My commandments that shine above the Dayspring of My creation.

Think not that We have revealed unto you a mere code of laws. Nay, rather, We have unsealed the choice Wine with the fingers of might and power. To this beareth witness that which the Pen of Revelation hath revealed. Meditate upon this, O men of insight!   Bahá'u'lláh, *Synopsis and Codification* of the *Kitáb-i-Aqdas*, p. 12

May 14

Whenever My laws appear like the sun in the heaven of Mine utterance, they must be faithfully obeyed by all, though My decree be such as to cause the heaven of every religion to be cleft asunder. He doth what he pleaseth. He chooseth; and none may question His choice. Whatsoever He, the Well-Beloved, ordaineth, the same is, verily, beloved. To this He Who is the Lord of all creation beareth Me witness. Whoso hath inhaled the sweet fragrance of the All-Merciful, and recognized the Source of this utterance, will welcome with his own eyes the shafts of the enemy, that he may establish the truth of the laws of God amongst men. Well is it with him that hath turned thereunto, and apprehended the meaning of His decisive decree.

Bahá'u'lláh, *Synopsis and Codification*
of the *Kitáb-i-Aqdas*, p. 12-13

May 15

The Great Being saith: O well-beloved ones! The tabernacle of unity hath been raised; regard ye not one another as strangers. Ye are the fruits of one tree, and the leaves of one branch. We cherish the hope that the light of justice may shine upon the world and sanctify it from tyranny. . . . There can be no doubt whatever that if the day star of justice, which the clouds of tyranny have obscured, were to shed its light upon men, the face of the earth would be completely transformed.

Bahá'u'lláh, *Tablets of Bahá'u'lláh*, p. 164

May 16

FEAST OF GRANDEUR

One holy soul is better than one thousand other souls. If a few souls gather together in a beloved meeting with the feelings of the Kingdom, with the divine attractions, with pure hearts and with absolute purity and holiness, to consort in spirit and fragrance, that gathering will have its effect upon all the world. The conditions, the words and the deeds of that gathering will lead a world to eternal happiness and will be an evidence of the favours of the Kingdom. The Holy Spirit will strengthen them and the hosts of the Supreme Concourse will render them victorious and the angels of Abhá will come in succession.
'Abdu'l-Bahá, *Bahá'í Meetings;*
The Nineteen Day Feast, pp. 5-6

May 17

O SON OF BEING!
My love is My stronghold; he that entereth therein is safe and secure, and he that turneth away shall surely stray and perish.

Bahá'u'lláh, *The Hidden Words of Bahá'u'lláh*,
No. 9 (Arabic)

May 18

Speak thou no word of politics; thy task concerneth the life of the soul, for this verily leadeth to man's joy in the world of God. Except to speak well of them, make thou no mention of the earth's kings, and the worldly governments thereof. Rather, confine thine utterance to spreading the blissful tidings of the Kingdom of God, and demonstrating the influence of the Word of God, and the holiness of the Cause of God. Tell thou of abiding joy and spiritual delights, and godlike qualities, and of how the Sun of Truth hath risen above the earth's horizons; tell of the blowing of the spirit of life into the body of the world.

'Abdu'l-Bahá, *Selections from the Writings of 'Abdu'l-Bahá*, pp. 92-93

May 19

O army of God! Beware lest ye harm any soul, or make any heart to sorrow; lest ye wound any man with your words, be he known to you or a stranger, be he friend or foe. Pray ye for all; ask ye that all be blessed, all be forgiven. Beware, beware, lest any of you seek vengeance, even against one who is thirsting for your blood. Beware, beware, lest ye offend the feelings of another, even though he be an evil-doer, and he wish you ill. Look ye not upon the creatures, turn ye to their Creator. See ye not the never-yielding people, see but the Lord of Hosts. Gaze ye not down upon the dust, gaze upward at the shining sun, which hath caused every patch of darksome earth to glow with light.

'Abdu'l-Bahá, *Selections from the Writings of 'Abdu'l-Bahá*, p. 73

May 20

Every man of discernment, while walking upon the earth, feeleth indeed abashed, inasmuch as he is fully aware that the thing which is the source of his prosperity, his wealth, his might, his exaltation, his advancement and power is, as ordained by God, the very earth which is trodden beneath the feet of all men. There can be no doubt that whoever is cognizant of this truth, is cleansed and sanctified from all pride, arrogance and vainglory.

Bahá'u'lláh, *Epistle to the Son of the Wolf*, p. 44

May 21

O thou who hast an illumined heart! Thou art even as the pupil of the eye, the very wellspring of the light, for God's love hath cast its rays upon thine inmost being and thou hast turned thy face toward the Kingdom of thy Lord.

Intense is the hatred, in America, between black and white, but my hope is that the power of the Kingdom will bind these two in friendship, and serve them as a healing balm.

Let them look not upon a man's colour but upon his heart. If the heart be filled with light, that man is nigh unto the threshold of His Lord; but if not, that man is careless of His Lord, be he white or be he black. 'Abdu'l-Bahá, *Selections from the Writings of 'Abdu'l-Bahá*, p. 113

May 22

In the world of humanity we find a great difference; the female sex is treated as though inferior, and is not allowed equal rights and privileges. This condition is due not to nature, but to education. In the Divine Creation there is no such distinction. Neither sex is superior to the other in the sight of God. Why then should one sex assert the inferiority of the other, withholding just rights and privileges as though God had given His authority for such a course of action? If women received the same educational advantages as those of men, the result would demonstrate the equality of capacity of both for scholarship.   'Abdu'l-Bahá, *Paris Talks*, p. 161

*THE ANNIVERSARY OF THE
DECLARATION OF THE BÁB BEGINS AT SUNSET.
IT SHOULD BE COMMEMORATED ABOUT
TWO HOURS AFTER SUNSET ON MAY 22*

May 23

I am, I am, I am the Promised One! I am the One Whose name you have for a thousand years invoked, at Whose mention you have risen, Whose advent you have longed to witness, and the hour of Whose Revelation you have prayed God to hasten. Verily, I say, it is incumbent upon the peoples of both the East and the West to obey My word, and to pledge allegiance to My person. The Báb, *God Passes By*, p. 21

May 24

They who dwell within the Tabernacle of God, and are established upon the seat of everlasting glory will refuse, though they be dying of hunger, to stretch their hands and seize unlawfully the property of their neighbour, however vile and worthless he may be.   Bahá'u'lláh, *The Advent of Divine Justice*, p. 19

May 25

If a man sleep, it should not be for pleasure, but to rest the body in order to do better, to speak better, to explain more beautifully, to serve the servants of God and to prove the truths. When he remains awake he should seek to be attentive, serve the Cause of God and sacrifice his own stations for those of God. When he attains to this station, the confirmations of the Holy Spirit will surely reach him, and man with this power can withstand all who inhabit the earth.

'Abdu'l-Bahá, *Pattern of Bahá'í Life*, p. 19

May 26

"I swear by My life! Nothing save that which profiteth them can befall My loved ones. To this testifieth the Pen of God, the Most Powerful, the All-Glorious, the Best Beloved." . . . "O my servants! Sorrow not if, in these days and on this earthly plane, things contrary to your wishes have been ordained and manifested by God, for days of blissful joy, of heavenly delight, are assuredly in store for you. Worlds, holy and spiritually glorious, will be unveiled to your eyes. You are destined by Him, in this world and hereafter, to partake of their benefits, to share in their joys, and to obtain a portion of their sustaining grace. To each and every one of them you will, no doubt, attain."

Bahá'u'lláh, *The Advent of Divine Justice*, p. 69

May 27

The civilization, so often vaunted by the learned exponents of arts and sciences, will, if allowed to overleap the bounds of moderation, bring great evil upon men. Thus warneth you He Who is the All-Knowing. If carried to excess, civilization will prove as prolific a source of evil as it had been of goodness when kept within the restraints of moderation. Meditate on this, O people, and be not of them that wander distraught in the wilderness of error. The day is approaching when its flame will devour the cities, when the Tongue of Grandeur will proclaim: "The Kingdom is God's, the Almighty, the All-Praised!" Bahá'u'lláh, *Gleanings from the Writings of Bahá'u'lláh*, pp. 342-343

May 28

Cast away, then, from you that which your minds abhor, for it hath been forbidden unto you in His Tablets and His Scriptures. Beware lest ye barter away the River that is life indeed for that which the souls of the pure-hearted detest. Become ye intoxicated with the wine of the love of God, and not with that which deadeneth your minds, O ye that adore Him! Verily it hath been forbidden unto every believer, whether man or woman.

Bahá'u'lláh, *The Advent of Divine Justice*, p. 27

The drinking of wine is, according to the text of the Most Holy Book, forbidden; for it is the cause of chronic diseases, weakeneth the nerves, and consumeth the mind.

'Abdu'l-Bahá, *The Advent of Divine Justice*, p. 27

THE ANNIVERSARY OF THE
ASCENSION OF BAHÁ'U'LLÁH BEGINS AT SUNSET.
IT SHOULD BE COMMEMORATED
AT 3 A.M. ON MAY 29

May 29

Let not your hearts be perturbed, O people, when the glory of My Presence is withdrawn, and the ocean of My utterance is stilled. In My presence amongst you there is a wisdom, and in My absence there is yet another, inscrutable to all but God, the Incomparable, the All-Knowing. Verily, We behold you from Our realm of glory, and shall aid whosoever will arise for the triumph of Our Cause with the hosts of the Concourse on high and a company of Our favoured angels.

Bahá'u'lláh, *Synopsis and Codification of the Kitáb-i-Aqdas*, p. 16

May 30

If we wish to pray, we must have some object on which to concentrate. If we turn to God, we must direct our hearts to a certain centre. If man worships God otherwise than through His Manifestation, he must first form a conception of God, and that conception is created by his own mind. As the finite cannot comprehend the Infinite, so God is not to be comprehended in this fashion. That which man conceives with his own mind he comprehends. That which he can comprehend is not God. That conception of God which a man forms for himself is but a phantasm, an image, an imagination, an illusion. There is no connection between such a conception and the Supreme Being.

'Abdu'l-Bahá, *Bahá'u'lláh and the New Era*, pp. 101-102

May 31

Prayers are granted through the universal Manifestations of God. Nevertheless, where the wish is to obtain material things, even where the heedless are concerned, if they supplicate, humbly imploring God's help—even their prayer hath an effect. . . .

. . . The prayers which were revealed to ask for healing apply both to physical and spiritual healing. Recite them, then, to heal both the soul and the body. If healing is right for the patient, it will certainly be granted; but for some ailing persons, healing would only be the cause of other ills, and therefore wisdom doth not permit an affirmative answer to the prayer.

. . . The power of the Holy Spirit healeth both physical and spiritual ailments.

'Abdu'l-Bahá, *Selections from the Writings of 'Abdu'l-Bahá*, pp. 161-162

June 1

Do ye not look upon the beginning of affairs; attach your hearts to the ends and results. The present period is like unto the sowing time. Undoubtedly it is impregnated with perils and difficulties, but in the future many a harvest shall be gathered, and benefits and results will become apparent. When one considers the issue and the end, inexhaustible joy and happiness will dawn.

Everything of importance in this world demands the close attention of its seeker. The one in pursuit of anything must undergo difficulties and hardships until the object in view is attained and the great success is obtained. This is the case of things pertaining to the world. How much higher is that which concerns the Supreme Concourse! That Cause involves every favour, glory and eternal bliss in the world of God.

'Abdu'l-Bahá, *The Divine Art of Living*, p. 92

June 2

The Call of God, when raised, breathed a new life into the body of mankind, and infused a new spirit into the whole creation. It is for this reason that the world hath been moved to its depths, and the hearts and consciences of men been quickened. Erelong the evidences of this regeneration will be revealed, and the fast asleep will be awakened.

'Abdu'l-Bahá, *The World Order of Bahá'u'lláh*, p. 169

June 3

Arts, crafts and sciences uplift the world of being, and are conducive to its exaltation. Knowledge is as wings to man's life, and a ladder for his ascent. Its acquisition is incumbent upon everyone. The knowledge of such sciences, however, should be acquired as can profit the peoples of the earth, and not those which begin with words and end with words. . . .

In truth, knowledge is a veritable treasure for man, and a source of glory, of bounty, of joy, of exaltation, of cheer and gladness unto him. Happy the man that cleaveth unto it, and woe betide the heedless.

Bahá'u'lláh, *Epistle to the Son of the Wolf*, pp. 26-27

June 4

In every cycle and dispensation, the feast hath been favoured and loved, and the spreading of a table for the lovers of God hath been considered a praiseworthy act. This is especially the case today, in this dispensation beyond compare, this most generous of ages, when it is highly acclaimed, for it is truly accounted among such gatherings as are held to worship and glorify God. Here the holy verses, the heavenly odes and laudations are intoned, and the heart is quickened, and carried away from itself.

The primary intent is to kindle these stirrings of the spirit, but at the same time it follows quite naturally that those present should partake of food, so that the world of the body may mirror the spirit's world, . . . 'Abdu'l-Bahá, *Selections from the Writings of 'Abdu'l-Bahá*, pp. 90-91

June 5

O SON OF SPIRIT!

I created thee rich, why dost thou bring thyself down to poverty? Noble I made thee, wherewith dost thou abase thyself? Out of the essence of knowledge I gave thee being, why seekest thou enlightenment from anyone beside Me? Out of the clay of love I molded thee, how dost thou busy thyself with another? Turn thy sight unto thyself, that thou mayest find Me standing within thee, mighty, powerful and self-subsisting.

Bahá'u'lláh, *The Hidden Words of Bahá'u'lláh*,
No. 13 (Arabic)

June 6

Blessed is he who in the prime of his youth and the heyday of his life will arise to serve the Cause of the Lord of the beginning and of the end, and adorn his heart with His love. The manifestation of such a grace is greater than the creation of the heavens and of the earth. Blessed are the steadfast and well is it with those who are firm.

Bahá'u'lláh, cited by the Universal House of Justice,
Message to the Bahá'ís of the World, Riḍván 1982

June 7

"The movement itself from place to place, when undertaken for the sake of God, hath always exerted, and can now exert, its influence in the world. In the Books of old the station of them that have voyaged far and near in order to guide the servants of God hath been set forth and written down." . . . "Whoso openeth his lips in this day, and maketh mention of the name of his Lord, the hosts of Divine inspiration shall descend upon him from the heaven of My name, the All-Knowing, the All-Wise. On him shall also descend the Concourse on high, each bearing aloft a chalice of pure light. Thus hath it been foreordained in the realm of God's Revelation, by the behest of Him Who is the All-Glorious, the Most Powerful."

Bahá'u'lláh, *The Advent of Divine Justice*, pp. 70-71

June 8

"He hath chosen out of the whole world the hearts of His servants, and made them each a seat for the revelation of His glory. Wherefore, sanctify them from every defilement, that the things for which they were created may be engraven upon them. This indeed is a token of God's bountiful favour." "Say, He is not to be numbered with the people of Bahá who followeth his mundane desires, or fixeth his heart on things of the earth. He is my true follower who, if he come to a valley of pure gold will pass straight through it aloof as a cloud, and will neither turn back, nor pause. Such a man is assuredly of Me. From his garment the Concourse on high can inhale the fragrance of sanctity."

Bahá'u'lláh, *The Advent of Divine Justice*, pp. 26

June 9

"It behooveth the people of Bahá to die to the world and all that is therein, to be so detached from all earthly things that the inmates of Paradise may inhale from their garment the sweet smelling savour of sanctity. . . . They that have tarnished the fair name of the Cause of God by following the things of the flesh—these are in palpable error!" "Purity and chastity have been, and still are, the most great ornaments for the handmaidens of God. God is My Witness! The brightness of the light of chastity sheddeth its illumination upon the worlds of the spirit, and its fragrance is wafted even unto the Most Exalted Paradise." "God hath verily made chastity to be a crown for the heads of His handmaidens. Great is the blessedness of that handmaiden that hath attained unto this great station."

Bahá'u'lláh, The Advent of Divine Justice, p. 27

June 10

In this new and wondrous dispensation the veils of superstition have been torn asunder and the prejudices of eastern peoples stand condemned. Among certain nations of the East, music was considered reprehensible, but in this new age the Manifest Light hath, in His holy Tablets, specifically proclaimed that music, sung or played, is spiritual food for soul and heart.

The musician's art is among those arts worthy of the highest praise, and it moveth the hearts of all who grieve. Wherefore, . . . play and sing out the holy words of God with wondrous tones in the gatherings of the friends, that the listener may be freed from chains of care and sorrow, and his soul may leap for joy and humble itself in prayer to the realm of Glory. 'Abdu'l-Bahá, *Selections from the Writings of 'Abdu'l-Bahá*, p. 112

June 11

Strive with heart and soul in order to bring about union and harmony among the white and the black and prove thereby the unity of the Bahá'í world wherein distinction of colour findeth no place, but where hearts only are considered. Praise be to God, the hearts of the friends are united and linked together, whether they be from the east or the west, from north or from south, whether they be German, French, Japanese, American, and whether they pertain to the white, the black, the red, the yellow or the brown race. Variations of colour, of land and of race are of no importance in the Bahá'í Faith; on the contrary, Bahá'í unity overcometh them all and doth away with all these fancies and imaginations.

'Abdu'l-Bahá, *Selections from the Writings of 'Abdu'l-Bahá*, pp. 112-113

June 12

My God, my God! If none be found to stray from Thy path, how, then, can the ensign of Thy mercy be unfurled, or the banner of Thy bountiful favour be hoisted? And if iniquity be not committed, what is it that can proclaim Thee to be the Concealer of men's sins, the Ever-Forgiving, the Omniscient, the All-Wise? May my soul be a sacrifice to the trespasses of them that trespass against Thee, for upon such trespasses are wafted the sweet savours of the tender mercies of Thy Name, the Compassionate, the All-Merciful. . . . May my inmost being be offered up for the sins of them that have sinned against Thee, for it is as a result of such sins that the Day Star of Thy manifold favours revealeth itself above the horizon of Thy bounty, and the clouds of Thy never-failing providence rain down their gifts upon the realities of all created things.

Bahá'u'lláh, *Gleanings from the Writings of Bahá'u'lláh*, pp. 310-311

June 13

There is no paradise more wondrous for any soul than to be exposed to God's Manifestation in His Day, to hear His verses and believe in them, to attain His presence, which is naught but the presence of God, to sail upon the sea of the heavenly kingdom of His good-pleasure, and to partake of the choice fruits of the paradise of His divine Oneness.

The Báb, *Selections from the Writings of the Báb*, p. 77

June 14

Know thou that when the Son of Man [Jesus Christ] yielded up His breath to God, the whole creation wept with a great weeping. By sacrificing Himself, however, a fresh capacity was infused into all created things. . . . The deepest wisdom which the sages have uttered, the profoundest learning which any mind hath unfolded, the arts which the ablest hands have produced, the influence exerted by the most potent of rulers, are but manifestations of the quickening power released by His transcendent, His all-pervasive and resplendent Spirit. We testify that when He came into the world, He shed the splendour of His glory upon all created things. Through Him the leper recovered from the leprosy of perversity and ignorance. Through Him the unchaste and wayward were healed. Through His power, born of Almighty God, the eyes of the blind were opened, and the soul of the sinner sanctified . . .

Bahá'u'lláh, *The World Order of Bahá'u'lláh*, pp. 185-186

June 15

What result is forthcoming from material rest, tranquillity, luxury and attachment to this corporeal world! It is evident that the man who pursues these things will in the end become afflicted with regret and loss.

Consequently, one must close his eyes wholly to these thoughts, long for eternal life, the sublimity of the world of humanity, the celestial developments, the Holy Spirit, the promotion of the Word of God, the guidance of the inhabitants of the globe, the promulgation of Universal Peace and the proclamation of the oneness of the world of humanity! *This is the work!* Otherwise like unto other animals and birds one must occupy himself with the requirements of this physical life, the satisfaction of which is the highest aspiration of the animal kingdom, and one must stalk across the earth like unto the quadrupeds. 'Abdu'l-Bahá, *Tablets of the Divine Plan*, p. 42

June 16

The time is at hand when whatsoever lieth hid in the souls and hearts of men will be disclosed. This Day is the Day . . . which the Lord of Glory announced and with which He acquainted Him Who was His Friend (Muhammad) through these, His words—exalted be He:—"O my son! Verily, God will bring everything to light, though it were but the weight of a grain of mustard-seed, and hidden in a rock or in the heavens or in the earth; for God is Subtle, informed of all." This Day the deceitful of eye, and all that men's breasts conceal, are made known and laid bare before the throne of His Revelation. Nothing whatsoever can escape His knowledge. He heareth and seeth, and He, in truth, is the All-Hearing, the All-Seeing. How very strange that they discern not between the trustworthy and the treacherous!

Bahá'u'lláh, *Epistle to the Son of the Wolf*, p. 107

June 17

It is clear and evident that the object of all preceding Dispensations hath been to pave the way for the advent of Muhammad, the Apostle of God. These, including the Muhammadan Dispensation, have had, in their turn, as their objective the Revelation proclaimed by the Qá'im [i.e. the Báb]. The purpose underlying this Revelation, as well as those that preceded it, has, in like manner, been to announce the advent of the Faith of Him Whom God will make manifest. And this Faith—the Faith of Him Whom God will make manifest—in its turn, together with all the Revelations gone before it, have as their object the Manifestation destined to succeed it. . . . The process of the rise and setting of the Sun of Truth will thus indefinitely continue—a process that hath had no beginning and will have no end.   The Báb, *The World Order of Bahá'u'lláh*, p. 117

June 18

And now concerning thy question whether human souls continue to be conscious one of another after their separation from the body. Know thou that the souls of the people of Bahá, who have entered and been established within the Crimson Ark, shall associate and commune intimately one with another, and shall be so closely associated in their lives, their aspirations, their aims and strivings as to be even as one soul. They are indeed the ones who are well-informed, who are keen-sighted, and who are endued with understanding. Thus hath it been decreed by Him Who is the All-Knowing, the All-Wise.

Bahá'u'lláh, *Gleanings from the Writings of Bahá'u'lláh*, pp. 169-170

June 19

The people of Bahá, who are the inmates of the Ark of God, are, one and all, well aware of one another's state and condition, and are united in the bonds of intimacy and fellowship. Such a state, however, must depend upon their faith and their conduct. They that are of the same grade and station are fully aware of one another's capacity, character, accomplishments and merits. They that are of a lower grade, however, are incapable of comprehending adequately the station, or of estimating the merits, of those that rank above them. Each shall receive his share from thy Lord. Blessed is the man that hath turned his face towards God, and walked steadfastly in His love, until his soul hath winged its flight unto God, the Sovereign Lord of all, the Most Powerful, the Ever-Forgiving, the All-Merciful.

Bahá'u'lláh, *Gleanings from the Writings of Bahá'u'lláh*, p. 170

June 20

Say: Teach ye the Cause of God, O people of Bahá, for God hath prescribed unto every one the duty of proclaiming His Message, and regardeth it as the most meritorious of all deeds. Such a deed is acceptable only when he that teacheth the Cause is already a firm believer in God, the Supreme Protector, the Gracious, the Almighty. He hath, moreover, ordained that His Cause be taught through the power of men's utterance, and not through resort to violence. Thus hath His ordinance been sent down from the Kingdom of Him Who is the Most Exalted, the All-Wise.

Bahá'u'lláh, *Gleanings from the Writings of Bahá'u'lláh*, p. 278

June 21

The All-Knowing Physician hath His finger on the pulse of mankind. He perceiveth the disease, and prescribeth, in His unerring wisdom, the remedy. Every age hath its own problem, and every soul its particular aspiration. The remedy the world needeth in its present-day afflictions can never be the same as that which a subsequent age may require. Be anxiously concerned with the needs of the age ye live in, and centre your deliberations on its exigencies and requirements.

Bahá'u'lláh, *Gleanings from the Writings of Bahá'u'lláh*, p. 213

June 22

Whoso layeth claim to a Revelation direct from God, ere the expiration of a full thousand years, such a man is assuredly a lying imposter. We pray God that He may graciously assist him to retract and repudiate such claim. Should he repent, God will, no doubt, forgive him. If, however, he persisteth in his error, God will, assuredly, send down one who will deal mercilessly with him. Terrible, indeed, is God in punishing! Whosoever interpreteth this verse otherwise than its obvious meaning is deprived of the Spirit of God and of His mercy which encompasseth all created things. Fear God, and follow not your idle fancies. Nay, rather follow the bidding of your Lord, the Almighty, the All-Wise.

Bahá'u'lláh, *Gleanings from the Writings of Bahá'u'lláh*, p. 346

June 23

FEAST OF MERCY

I charge you all that each one of you concentrate all the thoughts of your heart on love and unity. When a thought of war comes oppose it by a stronger thought of peace. A thought of hatred must be destroyed by a more powerful thought of love. Thoughts of war bring destruction to all harmony, well-being, restfulness and content. Thoughts of love are constructive of brotherhood, peace, friendship and happiness. . . .

If you desire with all your heart friendship with every race on earth, your thought, spiritual and positive, will spread; it will become the desire of others, growing stronger and stronger, until it reaches the minds of all men.

'Abdu'l-Bahá, *The Divine Art of Living*, p. 111

THE MONTH OF MERCY
BEGINS AT SUNSET

101

June 24

O SON OF MAN!

Thou art My dominion and My dominion perisheth not, wherefore fearest thou thy perishing? Thou art My light and My light shall never be extinguished, why dost thou dread extinction? Thou art My glory and My glory fadeth not; thou art My robe and My robe shall never be outworn. Abide then in thy love for Me, that thou mayest find Me in the realm of glory.

Bahá'u'lláh, *The Hidden Words of Bahá'u'lláh*,
No. 14 (Arabic)

June 25

It is enjoined upon every one of you to engage in some form of occupation, such as crafts, trades and the like. We have graciously exalted your engagement in such work to the rank of worship unto God, the True One. Ponder ye in your hearts the grace and the blessings of God and render thanks unto Him at eventide and at dawn. Waste not your time in idleness and sloth. Occupy yourselves with that which profiteth yourselves and others. . . .

The most despised of men in the sight of God are those who sit idly and beg. Hold ye fast unto the cord of material means, placing your whole trust in God, the Provider of all means. When anyone occupieth himself in a craft or trade, such occupation itself is regarded in the estimation of God as an act of worship; and this is naught but a token of His infinite and all-pervasive bounty.

Bahá'u'lláh, *Tablets of Bahá'u'lláh*, p. 26

June 26

In this Revelation the hosts that can render it victorious are the hosts of praiseworthy deeds and upright character. The leader and commander of these hosts hath ever been the fear of God, a fear that encompasseth all things and reigneth over all things.

Bahá'u'lláh, *Tablets of Bahá'u'lláh*, p. 126

June 27

In accordance with the divine teachings in this glorious Dispensation we should not belittle anyone and call him ignorant, saying: "You know not but I know." Rather, we should look upon others with respect, and when attempting to explain and demonstrate, we should speak as if we are investigating the truth, saying: "Here these things are before us. Let us investigate to determine where and in what form the truth can be found."

The teacher should not consider himself as learned and others ignorant. Such a thought breeds pride, and pride is unconducive to influence. The teacher should not see in himself any superiority; he should speak with the utmost kindliness, lowliness and humility, for such speech exerts influence and educates the souls.

'Abdu'l-Bahá, *The Individual and Teaching:*
Raising the Divine Call, p. 11

June 28

"Naught is seen in My temple but the Temple of God, and in My beauty but His Beauty, and in My being but His Being, and in My self but His Self, and in My movement but His Movement, and in My acquiescence but His Acquiescence, and in My pen but His Pen, the Mighty, the All-Praised. There hath not been in My soul but the Truth, and in Myself naught could be seen but God." "The Holy Spirit Itself hath been generated through the agency of a single letter revealed by this Most Great Spirit, if ye be of them that comprehend."

Bahá'u'lláh, *The World Order of Bahá'u'lláh*, p. 109

June 29

The root cause of wrongdoing is ignorance, and we must therefore hold fast to the tools of perception and knowledge. Good character must be taught. Light must be spread afar, so that, in the school of humanity, all may acquire the heavenly characteristics of the spirit, and see for themselves beyond any doubt that there is no fiercer hell, no more fiery abyss, than to possess a character that is evil and unsound; no more darksome pit nor loathsome torment than to show forth qualities which deserve to be condemned.

The individual must be educated to such a high degree that he would rather have his throat cut than tell a lie, and would think it easier to be slashed with a sword or pierced with a spear than to utter calumny or be carried away by wrath.

'Abdu'l-Bahá, *Selections from the Writings of 'Abdu'l-Bahá*, p. 136

June 30

It is the bounden duty of parents to rear their children to be staunch in faith, the reason being that a child who removeth himself from the religion of God will not act in such a way as to win the good pleasure of his parents and his Lord. For every praiseworthy deed is born out of the light of religion, and lacking this supreme bestowal the child will not turn away from any evil, nor will he draw nigh unto any good. Bahá'u'lláh, *Bahá'í Education*, p. 6

July 1

. . . a father and mother endure the greatest troubles and hardships for their children; and often when the children have reached the age of maturity, the parents pass on to the other world. Rarely does it happen that a father and mother in this world see the reward of the care and trouble they have undergone for their children. Therefore, children, in return for this care and trouble, must show forth charity and beneficence, and must implore pardon and forgiveness for their parents. So you ought, in return for the love and kindness shown you by your father, to give to the poor for his sake, with greatest submission and humility implore pardon and remission of sins, and ask for the supreme mercy.

'Abdu'l-Bahá, *Some Answered Questions*, pp. 231-232

July 2

The wisdom of prayer is this, that it causes a connection between the servant and the True One, because in that state of prayer man with all his heart and soul turns his face towards His Highness the Almighty, seeking His association and desiring His love and compassion. The greatest happiness for a lover is to converse with his beloved, and the greatest gift for a seeker is to become familiar with the object of his longing. That is why the greatest hope of every soul who is attracted to the kingdom of God is to find an opportunity to entreat and supplicate at the ocean of His utterance, goodness and generosity.

Besides all this, prayer and fasting is the cause of awakening and mindfulness and is conducive to protection and preservation from tests.

'Abdu'l-Bahá, *The Divine Art of Living*, p. 27

July 3

Some men's lives are solely occupied with the things of this world; their minds are so circumscribed by exterior manners and traditional interests that they are blind to any other realm of existence, to the spiritual significance of all things. . . . Like the animal, they have no thought beyond their own physical well-being. It is true that these necessities must be dispatched. Life is a load which must be carried on while we are on earth, but the cares of the lower things of life should not be allowed to monopolize all the thoughts and aspirations of a human being. The heart's ambitions should ascend to a more glorious goal, mental activity should rise to higher levels. Men should hold in their souls the vision of celestial perfection, and there prepare a dwelling-place for the inexhaustible bounty of the divine spirit.   'Abdu'l-Bahá, *The Reality of Man*, pp. 14-15

July 4

As to spiritual happiness, this is the true basis of the life of man, for life is created for happiness, not for sorrow; for pleasure, not for grief. Happiness is life; sorrow is death. Spiritual happiness is life eternal. This is a light which is not followed by darkness. This is an honour which is not followed by shame. This is a life that is not followed by death. This is an existence that is not followed by annihilation. This great blessing and precious gift is obtained by man only through the guidance of God. . . .   'Abdu'l-Bahá, *The Divine Art of Living*, p. 18

July 5

Turn all your thoughts toward bringing joy to hearts. Beware! Beware! lest ye offend any heart. Assist the world of humanity as much as possible. Be the source of consolation to every sad one, assist every weak one, be helpful to every indigent one, care for every sick one, be the cause of glorification to every lowly one, and shelter those who are overshadowed by fear.

In brief, let each one of you be as a lamp shining forth with the light of the virtues of the world of humanity. Be trustworthy, sincere, affectionate and replete with chastity. Be illumined, be spiritual, be divine, be glorious, be quickened of God, be a Bahá'í.   'Abdu'l-Bahá, *The Promulgation of Universal Peace*,
(1982 edition) p. 453

July 6

Be fair to yourselves and to others, that the evidences of justice may be revealed, through your deeds, among Our faithful servants. Beware lest ye encroach upon the substance of your neighbour. Prove yourselves worthy of his trust and confidence in you, and withhold not from the poor the gifts which the grace of God hath bestowed upon you. He, verily, shall recompense the charitable, and doubly repay them for what they have bestowed. No God is there but Him. All creation and its empire are His. He bestoweth His gifts on whom He will, and from whom He will He withholdeth them. He is the Great Giver, the Most Generous, the Benevolent.

Bahá'u'lláh, *Gleanings from the Writings of Bahá'u'lláh*, p. 278

July 7

It is clear and evident that all men shall, after their physical death, estimate the worth of their deeds, and realize all that their hands have wrought. I swear by the Day Star that shineth above the horizon of Divine power! They that are the followers of the one true God shall, the moment they depart out of this life, experience such joy and gladness as would be impossible to describe, while they that live in error shall be seized with such fear and trembling, and shall be filled with such consternation, as nothing can exceed. Well is it with him that hath quaffed the choice and incorruptible wine of faith through the gracious favour and the manifold bounties of Him Who is the Lord of all Faiths.

Bahá'u'lláh, *Gleanings from the Writings*
of Bahá'u'lláh, p. 171

July 8

It is even possible that the condition of those who have died in sin and unbelief may become changed—that is to say, they may become the object of pardon through the bounty of God, not through His justice—for bounty is giving without desert, and justice is giving what is deserved. As we have power to pray for these souls here, so likewise we shall possess the same power in the other world, which is the Kingdom of God. Are not all the people in that world the creatures of God? Therefore, in that world also they can make progress.

'Abdu'l-Bahá, *Some Answered Questions*
(1981 edition), p. 232

THE ANNIVERSARY OF THE MARTYRDOM OF THE BÁB BEGINS AT SUNSET. IT SHOULD BE COMMEMORATED ON JULY 9 AT ABOUT NOON

July 9

Alas, alas, for the things which have touched Me! . . . In this mountain [Maku] I have remained alone, and have come to such a pass that none of those gone before Me have suffered what I have suffered, nor any transgressor endured what I have endured!   The Báb, *The Promised Day is Come*, p. 8

O Thou Remnant of God! I have sacrificed myself wholly for Thee; I have accepted curses for Thy sake, and have yearned for naught but martyrdom in the path of Thy love. Sufficient witness unto me is God, the Exalted, the Protector, the Ancient of Days.   The Báb, *Selections from the Writings of the Báb*, p. 59

July 10

This is the Day whereon the All-Merciful hath come down in the clouds of knowledge, clothed with manifest sovereignty. He well knoweth the actions of men. He it is Whose glory none can mistake, could ye but comprehend it. The heaven of every religion hath been rent, and the earth of human understanding been cleft asunder, and the angels of God are seen descending. Say: This is the Day of mutual deceit; whither do ye flee? The mountains have passed away, and the heavens have been folded together, and the whole earth is held within His grasp, could ye but understand it. Who is it that can protect you? None, by Him Who is the All-Merciful! None, except God, the Almighty, the All-Glorious, the Beneficent.

Bahá'u'lláh, *Gleanings from the Writings of Bahá'u'lláh*, pp. 45-46

July 11

Say: The heavens have been folded together, and the earth is held within His grasp, and the corrupt doers have been held by their forelock, and still they understand not. They drink of the tainted water, and know it not. Say: The shout hath been raised, and the people have come forth from their graves, and arising, are gazing around them. Some have made haste to attain the court of the God of Mercy, others have fallen down on their faces in the fire of Hell, while still others are lost in bewilderment. The verses of God have been revealed, and yet they have turned away from them. His proof hath been manifested, and yet they are unaware of it. And when they behold the face of the All-Merciful, their own faces are saddened, while they are disporting themselves.   Bahá'u'lláh, *Gleanings from the Writings of Bahá'u'lláh*, pp. 41-42

July 12

FEAST OF WORDS

. . . when you present yourselves in the meetings, before entering them, free yourselves from all that you have in your heart, free your thoughts and your minds from all else save God, and speak to your heart. That all may make this a gathering of love, make it the cause of illumination, make it a gathering of attraction of the hearts, surround this gathering with the Lights of the Supreme Concourse so that you may be gathered together with the utmost love.

O God! Dispel all those elements which are the cause of discord, and prepare for us all those things which are the cause of unity and accord! O God! Descend upon us Heavenly Fragrance and change this gathering into a gathering of Heaven! Grant to us every benefit and every food. Prepare for us the Food of Love! Give to us the Food of Knowledge! Bestow upon us the Food of Heavenly Illumination!

In your hearts remember these things, and then enter the Unity Feast.

'Abdu'l-Bahá, *Bahá'í Meetings; the Nineteen Day Feast*, p. 20

July 13

O SON OF MAN!
Be thou content with Me and seek no other helper. For none but Me can ever suffice thee.

Bahá'u'lláh, *The Hidden Words of Bahá'u'lláh*, No. 17 (Arabic)

July 14

O people of loyalty, O people of faithfulness, O people who are awakened by the Breath of God, O people who are inhaling the scent of life from the Spirit of God! The path hath become smooth, the way straightened, the carpet of the Kingdom is spread, the Tabernacle hath been elevated upon the Hill of Might, the powers of heaven have been shaken, the corners of the earth have quaked, the sun has been darkened, the moon ceased to give light, the stars have fallen, the nations of the earth have lamented, and the Son of Man hath come upon the clouds of heaven with power and great glory, and He hath sent His angels with the sound of the great trumpet, and no one knows the meaning of these emblems save the wise and informed.

Ye are the angels, if your feet be firm, your spirits rejoiced, your secret thoughts pure, your eyes consoled, your ears opened, your breasts dilated

with joy, and your souls gladdened, and if you arise
to assist the Covenant, to resist dissension and to be
attracted to the Effulgence! Verily, I say unto you
that the Word of God has assuredly been explained
and has become an evident sign and a strong and
solid proof, and its traces shall be spread in the East
and West, and to these all heads shall bow and all
souls shall submit and kneel down with their faces to
the ground.   'Abdu'l-Bahá, *Bahá'í World Faith*, p. 360

July 15

It is incumbent upon everyone to write his testament. It behoveth him to adorn its heading with the Most Great Name, to testify therein to the oneness of God as manifested in the Day-Spring of His revelation and to set forth such good deeds as he may wish to be realized, that these may stand as his testimony in the worlds of Revelation and of Creation and be as a treasure stored up with his Lord, the Protector, the Trusted One.

Bahá'u'lláh, *Kitáb-i-Aqdas*, cited by the
Universal House of Justice in a letter to the
National Spiritual Assembly of the United States
dated 24 August 1982.

July 16

The question of consultation is of the utmost importance, and is one of the most potent instruments conducive to the tranquility and felicity of the people. For example, when a believer is uncertain about his affairs, or when he seeketh to pursue a project or trade, the friends should gather together and devise a solution for him. He, in his turn, should act accordingly. Likewise in larger issues, when a problem ariseth, or a difficulty occurreth, the wise should gather, consult, and devise a solution. They should then rely upon the One true God, and surrender to His Providence, in whatever way it may be revealed, for divine confirmations will undoubtedly assist. Consultation, therefore, is one of the explicit ordinances of the Lord of mankind.

'Abdu'l-Bahá, *Consultation: A Compilation*, p. 7

July 17

The first condition [for consultation] is absolute love and harmony amongst the members of the assembly. They must be wholly free from estrangement and must manifest in themselves the Unity of God, . . . Should harmony of thought and absolute unity be non-existent, that gathering shall be dispersed and that assembly be brought to naught. The second condition:—They must when coming together turn their faces to the Kingdom on High and ask aid from the Realm of Glory. They must then proceed with the utmost devotion, courtesy, dignity, care and moderation to express their views. They must in every matter search out the truth and not insist upon their own opinion, for stubbornness and persistence in one's views will lead ultimately to discord and wrangling and the truth will remain hidden.   'Abdu'l-Bahá, *Bahá'í Administration*, pp. 22-23

July 18

O My servants! . . . With firm determination, with the whole affection of your heart, and with the full force of your words, turn ye unto Him, and walk not in the ways of the foolish. The world is but a show, vain and empty, a mere nothing, bearing the semblance of reality. Set not your affections upon it. Break not the bond that uniteth you with your Creator, and be not of those that have erred and strayed from His ways. Verily I say, the world is like the vapour in a desert, which the thirsty dreameth to be water and striveth after it with all his might, until when he cometh unto it, he findeth it to be mere illusion. It may, moreover, be likened unto the lifeless image of the beloved whom the lover hath sought and found, in the end, after long search and to his utmost regret, to be such as cannot "fatten nor appease his hunger."

Bahá'u'lláh, *Gleanings from the Writings of Bahá'u'lláh*, pp. 328-329

July 19

The first and foremost duty prescribed unto men, next to the recognition of Him Who is the Eternal Truth, is the duty of steadfastness in His Cause. Cleave thou unto it, and be of them whose minds are firmly fixed and grounded in God. No act, however meritorious, did or can ever compare unto it. It is the king of all acts, and to this thy Lord, the All-Highest, the Most Powerful, will testify.

Bahá'u'lláh, *Gleanings from the Writings of Bahá'u'lláh*, p. 290

July 20

O Friends of the Pure and Omnipotent God! To be pure and holy in all things is an attribute of the consecrated soul and a necessary characteristic of the unenslaved mind. The best of perfections is immaculacy and the freeing of oneself from every defect. Once the individual is, in every respect, cleansed and purified, then will he become a focal centre reflecting the Manifest Light.

First in a human being's way of life must be purity, then freshness, cleanliness, and independence of spirit. First must the stream bed be cleansed, then may the sweet river waters be led into it. Chaste eyes enjoy the beatific vision of the Lord and know what this encounter meaneth; a pure sense inhaleth the fragrances that blow from the rose gardens of His grace; a burnished heart will mirror forth the comely face of truth.   'Abdu'l-Bahá, *Selections from the Writings of 'Abdu'l-Bahá*, p. 146

July 21

. . . in every aspect of life, purity and holiness, cleanliness and refinement, exalt the human condition and further the development of man's inner reality. Even in the physical realm, cleanliness will conduce to spirituality, as the Holy Writings clearly state. And although bodily cleanliness is a physical thing, it hath, nevertheless, a powerful influence on the life of the spirit. It is even as a voice wondrously sweet, or a melody played: although sounds are but vibrations in the air which affect the ear's auditory nerve, and these vibrations are but chance phenomena carried along through the air, even so, see how they move the heart. A wondrous melody is wings for the spirit, and maketh the soul to tremble for joy. The purport is that physical cleanliness doth also exert its effect upon the human soul.

'Abdu'l-Bahá, *Selections from the Writings
of 'Abdu'l-Bahá*, p. 147

July 22

Whensoever the light of Manifestation of the King of Oneness settleth upon the throne of the heart and soul, His shining becometh visible in every limb and member. At that time the mystery of the famed tradition gleameth out of the darkness: "A servant is drawn unto Me in prayer until I answer him; and when I have answered him, I become the ear wherewith he heareth. . . ." For thus the Master of the house hath appeared within His home, and all the pillars of the dwelling are ashine with His light. And the action and effect of the light are from the Light-Giver; so it is that all move through Him and arise by His will.

Bahá'u'lláh, *The Seven Valleys and the Four Valleys*, p. 22

July 23

O Divine Providence! Bestow Thou in all things purity and cleanliness upon the people of Bahá. Grant that they be freed from all defilement, and released from all addictions. Save them from committing any repugnant act, unbind them from the chains of every evil habit, that they may live pure and free, wholesome and cleanly, worthy to serve at Thy Sacred Threshold and fit to be related to their Lord.

'Abdu'l-Bahá, *Selections from the Writings of 'Abdu'l-Bahá*, p. 149

July 24

The teaching work should under all conditions be actively pursued by the believers because divine confirmations are dependent upon it. Should a Bahá'í refrain from being fully, vigorously and wholeheartedly involved in the teaching work he will undoubtedly be deprived of the blessings of the Abhá Kingdom. Even so, this activity should be tempered with wisdom—not that wisdom which requireth one to be silent and forgetful of such an obligation, but rather that which requireth one to display divine tolerance, love, kindness, patience, a goodly character, and holy deeds. In brief, encourage the friends individually to teach the Cause of God and draw their attention to this meaning of wisdom mentioned in the writings, which is itself the essence of teaching the Faith—but all this to be done with the greatest tolerance, so that heavenly assistance and divine confirmation may aid the friends. 'Abdu'l-Bahá, *The Individual and Teaching: Raising the Divine Call*, p. 12

July 25

As to the fundamentals of teaching the Faith: know thou that delivering the Message can be accomplished only through goodly deeds and spiritual attributes, an utterance that is crystal clear and the happiness reflected from the face of that one who is expounding the Teachings. It is essential that the deeds of the teacher should attest the truth of his words. Such is the state of whoso doth spread abroad the sweet savours of God and the quality of him who is sincere in his faith.

Once the Lord hath enabled thee to attain this condition, be thou assured that He will inspire thee with words of truth, and will cause thee to speak through the breathings of the Holy Spirit.

'Abdu'l-Bahá, *Selections from the Writings of 'Abdu'l-Bahá*, p. 175

July 26

Say: Rejoice not in the things ye possess; tonight they are yours, tomorrow others will possess them. Thus warneth you He Who is the All-Knowing, the All-Informed. Say: Can ye claim that what ye own is lasting or secure? Nay! By Myself, the All-Merciful. The days of your life flee away as a breath of wind, and all your pomp and glory shall be folded up as were the pomp and glory of those gone before you. Reflect, O people! What hath become of your by-gone days, your lost centuries? Happy the days that have been consecrated to the remembrance of God, and blessed the hours which have been spent in praise of Him Who is the All-Wise. Bahá'u'lláh, *Gleanings from the Writings of Bahá'u'lláh*, p. 138

July 27

"By the sorrows which afflict the beauty of the All-Glorious! Such is the station ordained for the true believer that if to an extent smaller than a needle's eye the glory of that station were to be unveiled to mankind, every beholder would be consumed away in his longing to attain it. For this reason it hath been decreed that in this earthly life the full measure of the glory of his own station should remain concealed from the eyes of such a believer." "If the veil be lifted and the full glory of the station of those who have turned wholly towards God, and in their love for Him renounced the world, be made manifest, the entire creation would be dumbfounded."

Bahá'u'lláh, *The World Order of Bahá'u'lláh*, pp. 110-111

July 28

The fire that hath inflamed the heart of Bahá is fiercer than the fire that gloweth in thine heart, and His lamentation louder than thy lamentation. Every time the sin committed by any one amongst them was breathed in the Court of His Presence, the Ancient Beauty would be so filled with shame as to wish He could hide the glory of His countenance from the eyes of all men, for He hath, at all times, fixed His gaze on their fidelity, and observed its essential requisites.

The words thou hadst written have, as soon as they were read in My Presence, caused the ocean of My fidelity to surge within Me, and the breeze of My forgiveness to be wafted over thy soul, and the tree of My loving-kindness to overshadow thee, and the clouds of My bounty to rain down upon thee their gifts. I swear by the Day Star that shineth above the horizon of eternity, I sorrow for thee in thy grief, and lament with thee in thy tribulation. . . . I bear witness to the services thou hast rendered Me, and testify to the various troubles thou hast sustained for My sake. All the atoms of the earth declare My love for thee.

Bahá'u'lláh, *Gleanings from the Writings of Bahá'u'lláh*, pp. 309–310

July 29

"Know thou, of a truth, these great oppressions that have befallen the world are preparing it for the advent of the Most Great Justice." "Say, He hath appeared with that Justice wherewith mankind hath been adorned, and yet the people are, for the most part, asleep." "The light of men is Justice. Quench it not with the contrary winds of oppression and tyranny. The purpose of justice is the appearance of unity among men." . . . "The shame I was made to bear hath uncovered the glory with which the whole of creation had been invested, and through the cruelties I have endured, the day-star of justice hath manifested itself, and shed its splendour upon men."

Bahá'u'lláh, *The Advent of Divine Justice*, pp. 23-24

July 30

A twofold obligation resteth upon him who hath recognized the Day Spring of the Unity of God, and acknowledged the truth of Him Who is the Manifestation of His oneness. The first is steadfastness in His love, such steadfastness that neither the clamour of the enemy nor the claims of the idle pretender can deter him from cleaving unto Him Who is the Eternal Truth, a steadfastness that taketh no account of them whatever. The second is strict observance of the laws He hath prescribed—laws which He hath always ordained, and will continue to ordain, unto men, and through which the truth may be distinguished and separated from falsehood.

Bahá'u'lláh, *Gleanings from the Writings of Bahá'u'lláh*, pp. 289-290

July 31

FEAST OF PERFECTION

They who are the beloved of God, in whatever place they gather and whomsoever they may meet, must evince, in their attitude towards God, and in the manner of their celebration of His praise and glory, such humility and submissiveness that every atom of the dust beneath their feet may attest the depth of their devotion. The conversation carried by these holy souls should be informed with such power that these same atoms of dust will be thrilled by its influence. Bahá'u'lláh, *Gleanings from the Writings of Bahá'u'lláh*, p. 7

THE MONTH OF PERFECTION
BEGINS AT SUNSET

August 1

O SON OF MAN!
Breathe not the sins of others so long as thou art thyself a sinner. Shouldst thou transgress this command, accursed wouldst thou be, and to this I bear witness.

Bahá'u'lláh, *The Hidden Words of Bahá'u'lláh*, No. 27 (Arabic)

August 2

The mystery of sacrifice is a most great subject and is inexhaustible.

Briefly it is as follows: The moth is a sacrifice to the candle. The spring is a sacrifice to the thirsty one. The sincere lover is a sacrifice to the loved one. The point lies in this: He must wholly forget himself. . . . He must seek the good pleasure of the True One; desire the face of the True One; and walk in the Path of the True One. . . . This is the first station of sacrifice.

The second station of sacrifice is as follows: Man must become like unto the iron thrown within the furnace of fire. The qualities of iron, such as blackness, coldness and solidity, which belong to the earth, disappear and vanish, while the character-istics of fire, such as redness, glowing and heat, which belong to the Kingdom, become apparent and visible. Therefore iron hath sacrificed its qualities and grades to the fire, acquiring the virtues of that element. 'Abdu'l-Bahá, *The Divine Art of Living*, p. 73

August 3

Know thou, O handmaid, that in the sight of Bahá, women are accounted the same as men, and God hath created all humankind in His own image, and after His own likeness. That is, men and women alike are the revealers of His names and attributes, and from the spiritual viewpoint there is no difference between them. Whosoever draweth nearer to God, that one is the most favoured, whether man or woman. How many a handmaid, ardent and devoted, hath, within the sheltering shade of Bahá, proved superior to the men, and surpassed the famous of the earth.

The House of Justice, however, according to the explicit text of the Law of God, is confined to men; this for a wisdom of the Lord God's, which will ere long be made manifest as clearly as the sun at high noon.   'Abdu'l-Bahá, *Selections from the Writings of 'Abdu'l-Bahá*, pp. 79-80

August 4

O handmaid of God! . . . To the mothers must be given the divine Teachings and effective counsel, and they must be encouraged and made eager to train their children, for the mother is the first educator of the child. It is she who must, at the very beginning, suckle the new-born at the breast of God's Faith and God's Law, that divine love may enter into him even with his mother's milk, and be with him till his final breath.

. . . It is incumbent upon the Spiritual Assemblies to provide the mothers with a well-planned programme for the education of children, showing how, from infancy, the child must be watched over and taught. These instructions must be given to every mother to serve her as a guide, so that each will train and nurture her children in accordance with the Teachings.

'Abdu'l-Bahá, *Selections from the Writings of 'Abdu'l-Bahá*, p. 138

August 5

Regard the world as the human body which, though at its creation whole and perfect, hath been afflicted, through various causes, with grave disorders and maladies. Not for one day did it gain ease, nay its sickness waxed more severe, as it fell under the treatment of ignorant physicians, who gave full rein to their personal desires, and have erred grievously. And if, at one time, through the care of an able physician, a member of that body was healed, the rest remained afflicted as before. Thus informeth you the All-Knowing, the All-Wise. . . .

That which the Lord hath ordained as the sovereign remedy and mightiest instrument for the healing of all the world is the union of all its peoples in one universal Cause, one common Faith. This can in no wise be achieved except through the power of a skilled, an all-powerful and inspired Physician. This, verily, is the truth, and all else naught but error.
Bahá'u'lláh, *Gleanings from the Writings of Bahá'u'lláh*, p. 254-255

August 6

That which is of paramount importance for the children, that which must precede all else, is to teach them the oneness of God and the Laws of God. For lacking this, the fear of God cannot be inculcated, and lacking the fear of God an infinity of odious and abominable actions will spring up, and sentiments will be uttered that transgress all bounds . . .

The parents must exert every effort to rear their offspring to be religious, for should the children not attain this greatest of adornments, they will not obey their parents, which in a certain sense means that they will not obey God. Indeed, such children will show no consideration to anyone, and will do exactly as they please.

Bahá'u'lláh, *Bahá'í Education: A Compilation*, p. 6

August 7

The Word of God hath set the heart of the world afire; how regrettable if ye fail to be enkindled with its flame! Please God, ye will regard this blessed night as the night of unity, will knit your souls together, and resolve to adorn yourselves with the ornament of a goodly and praiseworthy character. . . . I swear by Him Who hath caused Me to reveal whatever hath pleased Him! Ye are better known to the inmates of the Kingdom on high than ye are known to your own selves. Think ye these words to be vain and empty? Would that ye had the power to perceive the things your Lord, the All-Merciful, doth see— things that attest the excellence of your rank, that bear witness to the greatness of your worth, that proclaim the sublimity of your station! God grant that your desires and unmortified passions may not hinder you from that which hath been ordained for you.

Bahá'u'lláh, *Gleanings from the Writings of Bahá'u'lláh*, pp. 316-317

August 8

They who are possessed of riches, . . . must have the utmost regard for the poor, for great is the honour destined by God for those poor who are steadfast in patience. By My life! There is no honour, except what God may please to bestow, that can compare to this honour. Great is the blessedness awaiting the poor that endure patiently and conceal their sufferings, and well is it with the rich who bestow their riches on the needy and prefer them before themselves.

Bahá'u'lláh, *Gleanings from the Writings of Bahá'u'lláh*, p. 202

August 9

Please God, the poor may exert themselves and strive to earn the means of livelihood. This is a duty which, in this most great Revelation, hath been prescribed unto every one, and is accounted in the sight of God as a goodly deed. Whoso observeth this duty, the help of the invisible One shall most certainly aid him. He can enrich, through His grace, whomsoever He pleaseth. He, verily, hath power over all things.   Bahá'u'lláh, *Gleanings from the Writings of Bahá'u'lláh*, pp. 202-203

August 10

How lofty is the station which man, if he but chooseth to fulfil his high destiny, can attain! To what depths of degradation he can sink, depths which the meanest of creatures have never reached! Seize, O friends, the chance which this Day offereth you, and deprive not yourselves of the liberal effusions of His grace. I beseech God that He may graciously enable every one of you to adorn himself, in this blessed Day, with the ornament of pure and holy deeds.   Bahá'u'lláh, *Gleanings from the Writings of Bahá'u'lláh*, p. 206

August 11

Training in morals and good conduct is far more important than book learning. A child that is cleanly, agreeable, of good character, well-behaved—even though he be ignorant—is preferable to a child that is rude, unwashed, ill-natured, and yet becoming deeply versed in all the sciences and arts. The reason for this is that the child who conducts himself well, even though he be ignorant, is of benefit to others, while an ill-natured, ill-behaved child is corrupted and harmful to others, even though he be learned. If, however, the child be trained to be both learned and good, the result is light upon light.

'Abdu'l-Bahá, *Selections from the Writings of 'Abdu'l-Bahá*, pp. 135-136

August 12

"Religion is the greatest of all means for the establishment of order in the world and for the peaceful contentment of all that dwell therein. The weakening of the pillars of religion hath strengthened the hands of the ignorant and made them bold and arrogant. Verily I say, whatsoever hath lowered the lofty station of religion hath increased the waywardness of the wicked, and the result cannot be but anarchy." "Religion is a radiant light and an impregnable stronghold for the protection and welfare of the peoples of the world, for the fear of God impelleth man to hold fast to that which is good, and shun all evil. Should the lamp of religion be obscured, chaos and confusion will ensue, and the lights of fairness, of justice, of tranquillity and peace cease to shine."

Bahá'u'lláh, *The World Order of Bahá'u'lláh*, pp. 186-187

August 13

I now assure thee, O servant of God, that, if thy mind become empty and pure from every mention and thought and thy heart attracted wholly to the Kingdom of God, forgetting all else besides God and coming into communion with the Spirit of God, then the Holy Spirit will assist thee with a power which will enable thee to penetrate all things, and a Dazzling Spark which enlightens all sides; a Brilliant Flame in the zenith of the heavens, will teach thee that which thou dost not know of the facts of the universe and of the divine doctrine. Verily, I say unto thee, every soul that ariseth today to guide others to the path of safety and infuse into them the Spirit of Life, the Holy Spirit will inspire that soul with evidences, proofs and facts, and the lights will shine upon it from the Kingdom of God.

'Abdu'l-Bahá, *The Divine Art of Living*, pp. 46-47

August 14

They that have forsaken their country in the path
of God and subsequently ascended unto His presence, such souls shall be blessed by the Concourse
on High and their names recorded by the Pen of
Glory among such as have laid down their lives as
martyrs in the path of God, the Help in Peril, the
Self-Subsistent.

Bahá'u'lláh, *Messages from the Universal
House of Justice 1968-1973*, p. 102

August 15

The day is approaching when all the peoples of the world will have adopted one universal language and one common script. When this is achieved, to whatsoever city a man may journey, it shall be as if he were entering his own home. These things are obligatory and absolutely essential. It is incumbent upon every man of insight and understanding to strive to translate that which hath been written into reality and action.

Bahá'u'lláh, *Gleanings from the Writings of Bahá'u'lláh*, pp. 249-25

August 16

As for the question regarding marriage under the Law of God: first thou must choose one who is pleasing to thee, and then the matter is subject to the consent of father and mother. Before thou makest thy choice, they have no right to interfere. . . .

Bahá'í marriage is the commitment of the two parties one to the other, and their mutual attachment of mind and heart. Each must, however, exercise the utmost care to become thoroughly acquainted with the character of the other, that the binding covenant between them may be a tie that will endure forever. Their purpose must be this: to become loving companions and comrades and at one with each other for time and eternity.

'Abdu'l-Bahá, *Selections from the Writings of 'Abdu'l-Bahá*, p. 118

August 17

O ye two believers in God! The Lord, peerless is He, hath made woman and man to abide with each other in the closest companionship, and to be even as a single soul. They are two helpmates, two intimate friends, who should be concerned about the welfare of each other.

If they live thus, they will pass through this world with perfect contentment, bliss, and peace of heart, and become the object of divine grace and favour in the Kingdom of heaven. But if they do other than this, they will live out their lives in great bitterness, longing at every moment for death, and will be shamefaced in the heavenly realm.

Strive, then, to abide, heart and soul, with each other as two doves in the nest, for this is to be blessed in both worlds.

'Abdu'l-Bahá, *Selections from the Writings of 'Abdu'l-Bahá*, p. 122

August 18

Consort with all men, O people of Bahá, in a spirit of friendliness and fellowship. If ye be aware of a certain truth, if ye possess a jewel, of which others are deprived, share it with them in a language of utmost kindliness and good-will. If it be accepted, if it fulfil its purpose, your object is attained. If any one should refuse it, leave him unto himself, and beseech God to guide him. Beware lest ye deal unkindly with him. A kindly tongue is the lodestone of the hearts of men. It is the bread of the spirit, it clotheth the words with meaning, it is the fountain of the light of wisdom and understanding.

Bahá'u'lláh, *Gleanings from the Writings of Bahá'u'lláh*, p. 289

August 19

FEAST OF NAMES

Be in perfect unity. Never become angry with one another. . . . Love the creatures for the sake of God and not for themselves. You will never become angry or impatient if you love them for the sake of God. Humanity is not perfect. There are imperfections in every human being, and you will always become unhappy if you look toward the people themselves. But if you look toward God you will love them and be kind to them, for the world of God is the world of perfection and complete mercy. Therefore, do not look at the shortcomings of anybody; see with the sight of forgiveness. The imperfect eye beholds imperfections. The eye that covers faults looks toward the Creator of souls. He created them, trains and provides for them, endows them with capacity and life, sight and hearing; therefore, they are the signs of His grandeur.

'Abdu'l-Bahá, *Promulgation of Universal Peace*,
(1982 edition), p. 93

THE MONTH OF NAMES
BEGINS AT SUNSET

August 20

O SON OF BEING!

Bring thyself to account each day ere thou art summoned to a reckoning; for death, unheralded, shall come upon thee and thou shalt be called to give account for thy deeds.

Bahá'u'lláh, *The Hidden Words of Bahá'u'lláh*, No. 31 (Arabic)

August 21

Know thou of a certainty that Love is the secret of God's holy Dispensation, the manifestation of the All-Merciful, the fountain of spiritual outpourings. Love is heaven's kindly light, the Holy Spirit's eternal breath that vivifieth the human soul. Love is the cause of God's revelation unto man, the vital bond inherent, in accordance with the divine creation, in the realities of things. Love is the one means that ensureth true felicity both in this world and the next. Love is the light that guideth in darkness, the living link that uniteth God with man, that assureth the progress of every illumined soul. Love is the most great law that ruleth this mighty and heavenly cycle, the unique power that bindeth together the divers elements of this material world, the supreme magnetic force that directeth the movements of the spheres in the celestial realms. Love revealeth with unfailing and limitless power the mysteries latent in the universe. Love is the spirit of life unto the adorned body of mankind, the establisher of true civilization in this mortal world, and the shedder of imperishable glory upon every high-aiming race and nation.

'Abdu'l-Bahá, *Selections from the Writings of 'Abdu'l-Bahá*, p. 27

August 22

Beseech ye the one true God to grant that ye may taste the savour of such deeds as are performed in His path, and partake of the sweetness of such humility and submissiveness as are shown for His sake. Forget your own selves, and turn your eyes towards your neighbour. Bend your energies to whatever may foster the education of men. Nothing is, or can ever be, hidden from God. If ye follow in His way, His incalculable and imperishable blessings will be showered upon you.

Bahá'u'lláh, *Gleanings from the Writings of Bahá'u'lláh*, p. 9

August 23

O ye servants of the Blessed Beauty! . . . It is clear that in this day, confirmations from the unseen world are encompassing all those who deliver the divine Message. Should the work of teaching lapse, these confirmations would be entirely cut off, since it is impossible for the loved ones of God to receive assistance unless they teach. . . .

Souls are inclined toward estrangement. Steps should first be taken to do away with this estrangement, for only then will the Word take effect. . . .

If every one of the friends should strive in this way to guide one soul aright, the number of believers will double every year; and this can be accomplished with prudence and wisdom, and no harm whatever would result therefrom.

'Abdu'l-Bahá, *Selections from the Writings of 'Abdu'l-Bahá*, pp. 264-265

August 24

The worst human quality and the most great sin is backbiting, more especially when it emanates from the tongues of the believers of God. If some means were devised so that the doors of backbiting could be shut eternally, and each one of the believers of God unsealed his lips in praise of others, then the teachings of His Holiness Bahá'u'lláh would be spread, the hearts illumined, the spirits glorified, and the human world would attain to everlasting felicity.   'Abdu'l-Bahá, *Bahá'u'lláh and the New Era*, p. 94

August 25

Verily the most necessary thing is contentment under all circumstances; by this one is preserved from morbid conditions and from lassitude. Yield not to grief and sorrow: they cause the greatest misery. Jealousy consumeth the body and anger doth burn the liver: avoid these two as you would a lion.   Bahá'u'lláh, *Bahá'u'lláh and the New Era*, p. 117

August 26

This is the Day when the loved ones of God should keep their eyes directed towards His Manifestation, and fasten them upon whatsoever that Manifestation may be pleased to reveal. Certain traditions of bygone ages rest on no foundations whatever, while the notions entertained by past generations, and which they have recorded in their books, have, for the most part, been influenced by the desires of a corrupt inclination. Thou dost witness how most of the commentaries and interpretations of the words of God, now current amongst men, are devoid of truth. Their falsity hath, in some cases, been exposed when the intervening veils were rent asunder. They themselves have acknowledged their failure in apprehending the meaning of any of the words of God.

Our purpose is to show that should the loved ones of God sanctify their hearts and their ears from the vain sayings that were uttered aforetime, and turn with their inmost souls to Him Who is the Day Spring of His Revelation, and to whatsoever things He hath manifested, such behaviour would be regarded as highly meritorious in the sight of God.

Bahá'u'lláh, *Gleanings from the Writings of Bahá'u'lláh*, pp. 171-172

August 27

They that have forsaken their country for the purpose of teaching Our Cause—these shall the Faithful Spirit strengthen through its power. A company of Our chosen angels shall go forth with them, as bidden by Him Who is the Almighty, the All-Wise. How great the blessedness that awaiteth him that hath attained the honour of serving the Almighty! By My life! No act, however great, can compare with it, except such deeds as have been ordained by God, the All-Powerful, the Most Mighty. Such a service is, indeed the prince of all goodly deeds, and the ornament of every goodly act.

Bahá'u'lláh, *Gleanings from the Writings of Bahá'u'lláh*, p. 334

August 28

Know thou of a certainty that the Unseen can in no wise incarnate His Essence and reveal it unto men. He is, and hath ever been, immensely exalted beyond all that can either be recounted or perceived. From His retreat of glory His voice is ever proclaiming: "Verily, I am God; there is none other God besides Me, the All-Knowing, the All-Wise. I have manifested Myself unto men, and have sent down Him Who is the Day Spring of the signs of My Revelation. . . ." He Who is everlastingly hidden from the eyes of men can never be known except through His Manifestation, and His Manifestation can adduce no greater proof of the truth of His Mission than the proof of His own Person.

Bahá'u'lláh, *Gleanings from the Writings of Bahá'u'lláh*, p. 49

August 29

In brief, O ye believers of God! The text of the Divine Book is this: If two souls quarrel and contend about a question of the Divine questions, differing and disputing, *both are wrong*. The wisdom of this incontrovertible law of God is this: That between two souls from amongst the believers of God, no contention and dispute may arise; that they may speak with each other with infinite amity and love. Should there appear the least trace of controversy, they must remain silent, and both parties must continue their discussions no longer, but ask the reality of the question from the Interpreter. This is the irrefutable command!

Upon you be Bahá El-Abhá!

'Abdu'l-Bahá, *Tablets of the Divine Plan*, p. 53

August 30

The purpose underlying the revelation of every heavenly Book, nay of every divinely-revealed verse, is to endue all men with righteousness and understanding, so that peace and tranquillity may be firmly established amongst them. Whatsoever instilleth assurance into the hearts of men, whatsoever exalteth their station or promoteth their contentment, is acceptable in the sight of God.

Bahá'u'lláh, *Gleanings from the Writings of Bahá'u'lláh*, p. 206

August 31

Blessed is the man who hath detached himself from all else but Me, hath soared in the atmosphere of My love, hath gained admittance into My Kingdom, gazed upon My realms of glory, quaffed the living waters of My bounty, hath drunk his fill from the heavenly river of My loving providence, acquainted himself with My Cause, apprehended that which I concealed within the treasury of My Words, and hath shone forth from the horizon of divine knowledge engaged in My praise and glorification. Verily, he is of Me. Upon him rest My mercy, My loving-kindness, My bounty and My glory.   Bahá'u'lláh, *Tablets of Bahá'u'lláh*, p. 17

September 1

Know thou that every soul is fashioned after the nature of God, each being pure and holy at his birth. Afterwards, however, the individuals will vary according to what they acquire of virtues or vices in this world. Although all existent beings are in their very nature created in ranks or degrees, for capacities are various, nevertheless every individual is born holy and pure, and only thereafter may he become defiled.

And further, although the degrees of being are various, yet all are good. Observe the human body, its limbs, its members, the eye, the ear, the organs of smell, of taste, the hands, the fingernails. Notwithstanding the differences among all these parts, each one within the limitations of its own being participateth in a coherent whole. If one of them faileth it must be healed, and should no remedy avail, that part must be removed.

'Abdu'l-Bahá, *Selections from the Writings of 'Abdu'l-Bahá*, p. 190

September 2

As the spirit of man after putting off this material form has an everlasting life, certainly any existing being is capable of making progress; therefore, it is permitted to ask for advancement, forgiveness, mercy, beneficence and blessings for a man after his death because existence is capable of progression. That is why in the prayers of Bahá'u'lláh forgiveness and remission of sins are asked for those who have died. Moreover, as people in this world are in need of God, they will also need Him in the other world. The creatures are always in need, and God is absolutely independent, whether in this world or in the world to come.

'Abdu'l-Bahá, *Some Answered Questions*
(1981 edition), p. 231

September 3

. . . although the loss of a son is indeed heart-breaking and beyond the limits of human endurance, yet one who knoweth and understandeth is assured that the son hath not been lost but, rather, hath stepped from this world into another, and she will find him in the divine realm. . . .

That beloved child addresseth thee from the hidden world: "O thou kind Mother, thank divine Providence that I have been freed from a small and gloomy cage and, like the birds of the meadows, have soared to the divine world—a world which is spacious, illumined, and ever gay and jubilant. . . . I have shaken off the mortal form and have raised my banner in this spiritual world. Following this separation is everlasting companionship. Thou shalt find me in the heaven of the Lord, immersed in an ocean of light." 'Abdu'l-Bahá, *Selections from the Writings of 'Abdul-Baha*, p. 201

September 4

As this physical frame is the throne of the inner temple, whatever occurs to the former is felt by the latter. In reality that which takes delight in joy or is saddened by pain is the inner temple of the body, not the body itself. Since this physical body is the throne whereon the inner temple is established, God hath ordained that the body be preserved to the extent possible, so that nothing that causeth repugnance may be experienced. The inner temple beholdeth its physical frame, which is its throne. Thus, if the latter is accorded respect, it is as if the former is the recipient. The converse is likewise true.

Therefore, it hath been ordained that the dead body should be treated with the utmost honour and respect.

The Báb, *Selections from the Writings of the Báb*, p. 95

September 5

By the righteousness of God! The world and its vanities, and its glory, and whatever delights it can offer, are all, in the sight of God, as worthless as, nay, even more contemptible than, dust and ashes. Would that the hearts of men could comprehend it! Wash yourselves thoroughly, O people of Bahá, from the defilement of the world, and of all that pertaineth unto it. God Himself beareth Me witness. The things of the earth ill beseem you. Cast them away unto such as may desire them, and fasten your eyes upon this most holy and effulgent Vision.

Bahá'u'lláh, *Gleanings from the Writings of Bahá'u'lláh*, p. 304

September 6

O peoples of the earth! By My life and by your own! This Wronged One hath never had, nor hath He now any desire for leadership. Mine aim hath ever been, and still is, to suppress whatever is the cause of contention amidst the peoples of the earth, and of separation amongst the nations, so that all men may be sanctified from every earthly attachment, and be set free to occupy themselves with their own interests. We entreat Our loved ones not to besmirch the hem of Our raiment with the dust of falsehood, neither to allow references to what they have regarded as miracles and prodigies to debase Our rank and station, or to mar the purity and sanctity of Our name.

Bahá'u'lláh, Epistle to the Son of the Wolf, pp. 32-33

September 7

Become as true brethren in the one and indivisible religion of God, free from distinction, for verily God desireth that your hearts should become mirrors unto your brethren in the Faith, so that ye find yourselves reflected in them, and they in you. This is the true Path of God, the Almighty, and He is indeed watchful over your actions.

The Báb, *Selections from the Writings of The Báb*, p. 56

September 8

O SON OF MAN!

Thou art My dominion and My dominion
perisheth not, wherefore fearest thou thy perishing?
Thou art My light and My light shall never be
extinguished, why dost thou dread extinction? Thou
art My glory and My glory fadeth not; thou art My
robe and My robe shall never be outworn. Abide
then in thy love for Me, that thou mayest find Me in
the realm of glory.

Bahá'u'lláh, *The Hidden Words of Bahá'u'lláh*,
No. 14 (Arabic)

September 9

Assuredly we are today living in the Days of God. These are the glorious days on the like of which the sun hath never risen in the past. These are the days which the people in bygone times eagerly expected. What hath then befallen you that ye are fast asleep? These are the days wherein God hath caused the Day-Star of Truth to shine resplendent. What hath then caused you to keep your silence? These are the appointed days which ye have been yearningly awaiting in the past—the days of the advent of divine justice. Render ye thanks unto God, O ye concourse of believers.

The Báb, *Selections from the Writings of the Báb*, p. 161

September 10

I swear by the righteousness of Thy Lord, the Lord of all created things, the Lord of all the worlds! Were a man to rear in this world as many edifices as possible and worship God through every virtuous deed which God's knowledge embraceth, and attain the presence of the Lord, and were he, even to a measure less than that which is accountable before God, to bear in his heart a trace of malice towards Me, all his deeds would be reduced to naught and he would be deprived of the glances of God's favour, become the object of His wrath and assuredly perish. For God hath ordained that all the good things which lie in the treasury of His knowledge shall be attained through obedience unto Me, and every fire recorded in His Book, through disobedience unto Me.

The Báb, *Selections from the Writings of the Báb*, p. 11

September 11

O ye spiritual friends! Such must be your constancy that should the evil-wishers put every believer to death and only one remain, that one, singly and alone, will withstand all the peoples of the earth, and will go on scattering far and wide the sweet and holy fragrances of God. Wherefore, should any fearsome news, any word of terrifying events, reach you from the Holy Land, see to it that ye waver not, be ye not stricken by grief, be ye not shaken. Rather, rise ye up instantly, with iron resolve, and serve ye the Kingdom of God.

'Abdu'l-Bahá, *Selections from the Writings of 'Abdu'l-Bahá*, pp. 78-79

September 12

O my beloved friends! You are the bearers of the name of God in this Day. You have been chosen as the repositories of His mystery. It behooves each one of you to manifest the attributes of God, and to exemplify by your deeds and words the signs of His righteousness, His power and glory. The very members of your body must bear witness to the loftiness of your purpose, the integrity of your life, the reality of your faith, and the exalted character of your devotion . . .

The days when idle worship was deemed sufficient are ended. The time is come when naught but the purest motive, supported by deeds of stainless purity, can ascend to the throne of the Most High and be acceptable unto Him . . .

The Báb, *The Dawn-Breakers*, pp. 92-93

September 13

O army of life! East and West have joined to worship stars of faded splendour and have turned in prayer unto darkened horizons. . . . They have regarded certain customs and conventions as the immutable basis of the Divine Faith, and have firmly established themselves therein. They have imagined themselves as having attained the glorious pinnacle of achievement and prosperity when in reality they have touched the innermost depths of heedlessness and deprived themselves wholly of God's bountiful gifts.

The corner-stone of the religion of God is the acquisition of the Divine perfections and the sharing in His manifold bestowals. The essential purpose of Faith and Belief is to ennoble the inner being of man with the outpourings of grace from on high. If this be not attained, it is indeed deprivation itself. It is the torment of infernal fire.

Wherefore it is incumbent upon all Bahá'ís to ponder this very delicate and vital matter in their hearts, that, unlike other religions, they may not content themselves with the noise, the clamour, the hollowness of religious doctrine. . . . For in this holy Dispensation, the crowning glory of bygone ages, and cycles, true Faith is no mere acknowledgement of the Unity of God, but the living of a life that will manifest all the perfections and virtues implied in such belief.

'Abdu'l-Bahá, *The Divine Art of Living*, pp. 24-25

September 14

"Be unrestrained as the wind while carrying the Message of Him Who hath caused the dawn of Divine Guidance to break. Consider how the wind, faithful to that which God hath ordained, bloweth upon all regions of the earth, be they inhabited or desolate. Neither the sight of desolation, nor the evidences of prosperity, can either pain or please it. It bloweth in every direction, as bidden by its Creator." "And when he determineth to leave his home, for the sake of the Cause of his Lord, let him put his whole trust in God, as the best provision for his journey, and array himself with the robe of virtue. . . . If he be kindled with the fire of His love, if he forgoeth all created things, the words he uttereth shall set on fire them that hear him."

Bahá'u'lláh, *The Advent of Divine Justice*, p. 42

September 15

The Third Tajallí (Effulgence)
is concerning arts, crafts and sciences. Knowledge
is as wings to man's life, and a ladder for his ascent.
Its acquisition is incumbent upon everyone. The
knowledge of such sciences, however, should be
acquired as can profit the peoples of the earth, and
not those which begin with words and end with
words. Great indeed is the claim of scientists and
craftsmen on the peoples of the world. Unto this
beareth witness the Mother Book on the day of His
return. Happy are those possessed of a hearing ear.
In truth, knowledge is a veritable treasure for man,
and a source of glory, of bounty, of joy, of
exaltation, of cheer and gladness unto him. Thus
hath the Tongue of Grandeur spoken in this Most
Great Prison. Bahá'u'lláh, *Tablets of Bahá'u'lláh*
pp. 51-52

September 16

O contending peoples and kindreds of the earth!
Set your faces towards unity, and let the radiance of
its light shine upon you. Gather ye together, and for
the sake of God resolve to root out whatever is the
source of contention amongst you. . . . There can be
no doubt whatever that the peoples of the world, of
whatever race or religion, derive their inspiration
from one heavenly Source, and are the subjects of
one God. The difference between the ordinances
under which they abide should be attributed to the
varying requirements and exigencies of the age in
which they were revealed. All of them, except a few
which are the outcome of human perversity, were
ordained of God, and are a reflection of His Will and
Purpose. Arise and, armed with the power of faith,
shatter to pieces the gods of your vain imaginings,
the sowers of dissension amongst you. Cleave unto
that which draweth you together and uniteth you.

Bahá'u'lláh, *Gleanings from the Writings
of Bahá'u'lláh*, p. 217

September 17

How great the number of people who deck themselves with robes of silk all their lives, while clad in the garb of fire, inasmuch as they have divested themselves of the raiment of divine guidance and righteousness; and how numerous are those who wear clothes made of cotton or coarse wool throughout their lives, and yet by reason of their being endowed with the vesture of divine guidance and righteousness, are truly attired with the raiment of Paradise and take delight in the good-pleasure of God. Indeed it would be better in the sight of God were ye to combine the two, adorning yourselves with the raiment of divine guidance and righteousness and wearing exquisite silk, if ye can afford to do so. If not, at least act ye not unrighteously, but rather observe piety and virtue . . .

The Báb, *Selections from the Writings of the Báb*, p. 149

September 18

Say: Let truthfulness and courtesy be your adorning. Suffer not yourselves to be deprived of the robe of forbearance and justice, that the sweet savours of holiness may be wafted from your hearts upon all created things. Say: Beware, O people of Baha, lest ye walk in the ways of them whose words differ from their deeds. Strive that ye may be enabled to manifest to the peoples of the earth the signs of God, and to mirror forth His command-ments. Let your acts be a guide unto all mankind, for the professions of most men, be they high or low, differ from their conduct. It is through your deeds that ye can distinguish yourselves from others.

Bahá'u'lláh, *Gleanings from the Writings
of Bahá'u'lláh*, p. 305

September 19

Pay ye no heed to aversion and rejection, to disdain, hostility, injustice: act ye in the opposite way. Be ye sincerely kind, not in appearance only. Let each one of God's loved ones centre his attention on this: to be the Lord's mercy to man; to be the Lord's grace. Let him do some good to every person whose path he crosseth, and be of some benefit to him. . . . In this way, the light of divine guidance will shine forth, and the blessings of God will cradle all mankind: for love is light, no matter in what abode it dwelleth; and hate is darkness, no matter where it may make its nest.

'Abdu'l-Bahá, *Selections from the Writings of 'Abdu'l-Bahá*, pp. 2-3

September 20

O ye rich ones of the earth! Flee not from the face of the poor that lieth in the dust, nay rather befriend him and suffer him to recount the tale of the woes with which God's inscrutable Decree hath caused him to be afflicted. By the righteousness of God! Whilst ye consort with him, the Concourse on high will be looking upon you, will be interceding for you, will be extolling your names and glorifying your action. Blessed are the learned that pride not themselves on their attainments; and well is it with the righteous that mock not the sinful, but rather conceal their misdeeds, so that their own shortcomings may remain veiled to men's eyes.

Bahá'u'lláh, *Gleanings from the Writings of Bahá'u'lláh*, pp. 314-315

September 21

At whatever time highly-skilled physicians shall have developed the healing of illnesses by means of foods, and shall make provision for simple foods, and shall prohibit humankind from living as slaves to their lustful appetites, it is certain that the incidence of chronic and diversified illnesses will abate, and the general health of all mankind will be much improved. This is destined to come about.

In the same way, in the character, the conduct and the manners of men, universal modifications will be made. 'Abdu'l-Bahá, *Selections from the Writings of 'Abdu'l-Bahá*, 156

September 22

This people have passed beyond the narrow straits of names, and pitched their tents upon the shores of the sea of renunciation. They would willingly lay down a myriad lives, rather than breathe the word desired by their enemies. They have clung to that which pleaseth God, and are wholly detached and freed from the things which pertain unto men. They have preferred to have their heads cut off rather than utter one unseemly word. Ponder this in thine heart. Methinks they have quaffed their fill of the ocean of renunciation. The life of the present world hath failed to withhold them from suffering martyrdom in the path of God.

Bahá'u'lláh, *Epistle to the Son of the Wolf*, p. 74

September 23

This people need no weapons of destruction, inasmuch as they have girded themselves to reconstruct the world. Their hosts are the hosts of goodly deeds, and their arms the arms of upright conduct, and their commander the fear of God. Blessed that one that judgeth with fairness. By the righteousness of God! Such hath been the patience, the calm, the resignation and contentment of this people that they have become the exponents of justice, and so great hath been their forbearance, that they have suffered themselves to be killed rather than kill, . . . What is it that could have induced them to reconcile themselves to these grievous trials, and to refuse to put forth a hand to repel them? What could have caused such resignation and serenity? The true cause is to be found in the ban which the Pen of Glory hath, day and night, chosen to impose, . . .

Bahá'u'lláh, *Epistle to the Son of the Wolf*, pp. 74-75

September 24

"Whatever hath befallen you, hath been for the sake of God. This is the truth, and in this there is no doubt. You should, therefore, leave all your affairs in His hands, place your trust in Him, and rely upon Him. He will assuredly not forsake you. In this, likewise, there is no doubt. No father will surrender his sons to devouring beasts; no shepherd will leave his flock to ravening wolves. He will most certainly do his utmost to protect his own.

"If, however, for a few days, in compliance with God's all-encompassing wisdom, outward affairs should run their course contrary to one's cherished desire, this is of no consequence and should not matter. Our intent is that all the friends should fix their gaze on the Supreme Horizon, and cling to that which hath been revealed in the Tablets."

Bahá'u'lláh
cited by The Universal House of Justice, December, 1983

September 25

There are certain pillars which have been established as the unshakeable supports of the Faith of God. The mightiest of these is learning and the use of the mind, the expansion of consciousness, and insight into the realities of the universe and the hidden mysteries of Almighty God.

To promote knowledge is thus an inescapable duty imposed on every one of the friends of God. It is incumbent upon that Spiritual Assembly, that assemblage of God, to exert every effort to educate the children, so that from infancy they will be trained in Bahá'í conduct and the ways of God, and will, even as young plants, thrive and flourish in the soft-flowing waters that are the counsels and admonitions of the Blessed Beauty.

'Abdu'l-Bahá, *Selections from the Writings of 'Abdu'l-Bahá*, p. 126

September 26

FEAST OF WILL

It is my hope that the Nineteen Day Feast may become firmly established and organized so that the holy realities which are behind this meeting may leave behind all prejudices and conflict, and make their hearts as a treasury of love. Even if there is the slightest feeling between certain souls—a lack of love—it must be made to entirely disappear. There must be the utmost translucency and purity of intention.

. . . When they gather in this meeting, all those present must turn their faces toward the Kingdom of Abhá, and from their hearts supplicate, invoke and entreat toward the lofty throne, beg of God's forgiveness for all shortcomings, read the teachings and arise to His service.

'Abdu'l-Bahá, *Bahá'í Meetings;*
The Nineteen Day Feast, pp. 21-22

THE MONTH OF WILL
BEGINS AT SUNSET

September 27

O SON OF MAN!
Neglect not My commandments if thou lovest My beauty, and forget not My counsels if thou wouldst attain My good pleasure.

Bahá'u'lláh, *The Hidden Words of Bahá'u'lláh*,
No. 39 (Arabic)

September 28

Proclaim the Cause of thy Lord unto all who are in the heavens and on the earth. Should any man respond to thy call, lay bare before him the pearls of the wisdom of the Lord, thy God, which His Spirit hath sent down upon thee, and be thou of them that truly believe. And should any one reject thy offer, turn thou away from him, and put thy trust and confidence in the Lord of all worlds. By the righteousness of God! Whoso openeth his lips in this day, and maketh mention of the name of his Lord, the hosts of Divine inspiration shall descend upon him from the heaven of my name, the All-Knowing, the All-Wise. On him shall also descend the Concourse on high, each bearing aloft a chalice of pure light. Thus hath it been fore-ordained in the realm of God's Revelation, by the behest of Him Who is the All-Glorious, the Most Powerful.

Bahá'u'lláh, *The Advent of Divine Justice*, p. 51

September 29

"Verily I say! No one hath apprehended the root of this Cause. It is incumbent upon every one, in this day, to perceive with the eye of God, and to hearken with His ear. Whoso beholdeth Me with an eye besides Mine own will never be able to know Me. None among the Manifestations of old, except to a prescribed degree, hath ever completely apprehended the nature of this Revelation." . . . "The purpose underlying all creation is the revelation of this most sublime, this most holy Day, the Day known as the Day of God, in His Books and Scriptures—the Day which all the Prophets, and the Chosen Ones, and the holy ones, have wished to witness."

Bahá'u'lláh, *The Advent of Divine Justice*, pp. 64-65

September 30

The second Tajallí (Effulgence)
is to remain steadfast in the Cause of God—
exalted be His glory—and to be unswerving in His
love. And this can in no wise be attained except
through full recognition of Him; and full recognition
cannot be obtained save by faith in the blessed
words: "He doeth whatsoever He willeth." Whoso
tenaciously cleaveth unto this sublime word and
drinketh deep from the living waters of utterance
which are inherent therein, will be imbued with such
a constancy that all the books of the world will be
powerless to deter him from the Mother Book.

Bahá'u'lláh, *Tablets of Bahá'u'lláh*, p. 51

October 1

My imprisonment doeth Me no harm, neither the tribulations I suffer, nor the things that have befallen Me at the hands of My oppressors. That which harmeth Me is the conduct of those who, though they bear My name, yet commit that which maketh My heart and My pen to lament. They that spread disorder in the land, and lay hands on the property of others, and enter a house without leave of its owner, We, verily, are clear of them, unless they repent and return unto God, the Ever-Forgiving, the Most Merciful.

Bahá'u'lláh, *Epistle to the Son of the Wolf*, p. 23

October 2

Today, humanity is bowed down with trouble, sorrow and grief, no one escapes; the world is wet with tears; but, thank God, the remedy is at our doors. Let us turn our hearts away from the world of matter and live in the spiritual world! It alone can give us freedom! If we are hemmed in by difficulties we have only to call upon God, and by His great Mercy we shall be helped. . . .

When our thoughts are filled with the bitterness of this world, let us turn our eyes to the sweetness of God's compassion and He will send us heavenly calm! If we are imprisoned in the material world, our spirit can soar into the Heavens and we shall be free indeed!   'Abdu'l-Bahá, *Paris Talks*, pp. 110-111

October 3

O thou servant of God! Do not grieve at the afflictions and calamities that have befallen thee. All calamities and afflictions have been created for man so that he may spurn this mortal world—a world to which he is much attached. When he experienceth severe trials and hardships, then his nature will recoil and he will desire the eternal realm—a realm which is sanctified from all afflictions and calamities. Such is the case with the man who is wise. He shall never drink from a cup which is at the end distasteful, but, on the contrary, he will seek the cup of pure and limpid water. He will not taste of the honey that is mixed with poison.

'Abdu'l-Bahá, *Selections from the Writings of 'Abdu'l-Bahá*, p. 239

October 4

Follow thou the way of thy Lord, and say not that which the ears cannot bear to hear, for such speech is like luscious food given to small children. However palatable, rare and rich the food may be, it cannot be assimilated by the digestive organs of a suckling child. Therefore unto every one who hath a right, let his settled measure be given.

"Not everything that a man knoweth can be disclosed, nor can everything that he can disclose be regarded as timely, nor can every timely utterance be considered as suited to the capacity of those who hear it." Such is the consummate wisdom to be observed in thy pursuits. Be not oblivious thereof, if thou wishest to be a man of action under all conditions. First diagnose the disease and identify the malady, then prescribe the remedy, for such is the perfect method of the skilful physician.

'Abdu'l-Bahá, *Selections from the Writings of 'Abdu'l-Bahá*, pp. 268-269

October 5

Act in accordance with the counsels of the Lord: that is, rise up in such wise, and with such qualities, as to endow the body of this world with a living soul, and to bring this young child, humanity, to the stage of adulthood. So far as ye are able, ignite a candle of love in every meeting, and with tenderness rejoice and cheer ye every heart. Care for the stranger as for one of your own; show to alien souls the same loving kindness ye bestow upon your faithful friends. Should any come to blows with you, seek to be friends with him; . . . Perchance such ways and words from you will make this darksome world turn bright at last; . . .

'Abdu'l-Bahá, *Selections from the Writings of 'Abdu'l-Bahá*, p. 34

October 6

The Great Being, wishing to reveal the pre-requisites of the peace and tranquillity of the world and the advancement of its peoples, hath written: The time must come when the imperative necessity for the holding of a vast, an all-embracing assemblage of men will be universally realized. The rulers and kings of the earth must needs attend it, and, participating in its deliberations, must consider such ways and means as will lay the foundations of the world's Great Peace amongst men. . . . Should any king take up arms against another, all should unitedly arise and prevent him. If this be done, the nations of the world will no longer require any armaments, except for the purpose of preserving the security of their realms and of maintaining internal order within their territories. This will ensure the peace and composure of every people, government and nation.   Bahá'u'lláh, *Gleanings from the Writings of Bahá'u'lláh*, p. 249

October 7

When the victory arriveth, every man shall profess himself as believer and shall hasten to the shelter of God's Faith. Happy are they who in the days of world-encompassing trials have stood fast in the Cause and refused to swerve from its truth.

Bahá'u'lláh, *Gleanings from the Writings of Bahá'u'lláh*, p. 319

October 8

The Báb hath said: "Should a tiny ant desire, in this day, to be possessed of such power as to be able to unravel the abstrusest and most bewildering passages of the Qur'án, its wish will no doubt be fulfilled, inasmuch as the mystery of eternal might vibrates within the innermost being of all created things." If so helpless a creature can be endowed with so subtle a capacity, how much more efficacious must be the power released through the liberal effusions of the grace of Bahá'u'lláh!

'Abdu'l-Bahá, *The Advent of Divine Justice*, p. 39

October 9

"O my friend! The undying Fire which the Lord of the Kingdom hath kindled in the midst of the holy Tree is burning fiercely in the midmost heart of the world. The conflagration it will provoke will envelop the whole earth. Its blazing flames will illuminate its peoples and kindreds. All the signs have been revealed; every prophetic allusion hath been manifested. . . ." "What more shall I say? What else can my pen recount? So loud is the call that reverberates from the Abhá Kingdom that mortal ears are well-nigh deafened with its vibrations. The whole creation, methinks, is being disrupted and is bursting asunder through the shattering influence of the Divine summons issued from the throne of glory."

'Abdu'l-Bahá, *The World Order of Bahá'u'lláh*, pp. 111-112

October 10

"The effulgence of God's splendrous mercy hath enveloped the peoples and kindreds of the earth, and the whole world is bathed in its shining glory . . . The day will soon come when the light of Divine unity will have so permeated the East and the West that no man dare any longer ignore it." "Now in the world of being the Hand of divine power hath firmly laid the foundations of this all-highest bounty and this wondrous gift. Whatsoever is latent in the innermost of this holy cycle shall gradually appear and be made manifest, for now is but the beginning of its growth and the day-spring of the revelation of its signs. Ere the close of this century and of this age, it shall be made clear and evident how wondrous was that springtide and how heavenly was that gift!"

'Abdu'l-Bahá, *The World Order of Bahá'u'lláh*, p. 111

October 11

The Book of God is wide open, and His Word is summoning mankind unto Him. No more than a mere handful, however, hath been found willing to cleave to His Cause, or to become the instruments for its promotion. These few have been endued with the Divine Elixir that can, alone, transmute into purest gold the dross of the world, and have been empowered to administer the infallible remedy for all the ills that afflict the children of men. No man can obtain everlasting life, unless he embraceth the truth of this inestimable, this wondrous, and sublime Revelation.

Bahá'u'lláh, *Gleanings from the Writings of Bahá'u'lláh*, p. 183

October 12

"Say: O people of God! Beware lest the powers of the earth alarm you, or the might of the nations weaken you, or the tumult of the people of discord deter you, or the exponents of earthly glory sadden you. Be ye as a mountain in the Cause of your Lord, the Almighty, the All-Glorious, the Unconstrained." . . . "I swear by My life! Nothing save that which profiteth them can befall My loved ones. To this testifieth the Pen of God, the Most Powerful, the All-Glorious, the Best Beloved." "Let not the happenings of the world sadden you. I swear by God! The sea of joy yearneth to attain your presence, for every good thing hath been created for you, and will, according to the needs of the times, be revealed unto you."

Bahá'u'lláh, *The Advent of Divine Justice*, p. 69

October 13

How great, how very great is the Cause! How very fierce the onslaught of all the peoples and kindreds of the earth. Ere long shall the clamour of the multitude throughout Africa, throughout America, the cry of the European and of the Turk, the groaning of India and China, be heard from far and near. One and all, they shall arise with all their power to resist His Cause. Then shall the knights of the Lord, assisted by His grace from on high, strengthened by faith, aided by the power of understanding, and reinforced by the legions of the Covenant, arise and make manifest the truth of the verse: "Behold the confusion that hath befallen the tribes of the defeated!"

'Abdu'l-Bahá, *The World Order of Bahá'u'lláh*, p. 17

October 14

"Through the movement of Our Pen of Glory We have, at the bidding of the Omnipotent Ordainer, breathed a new life into every human frame, and instilled into every word a fresh potency. All created things proclaim the evidences of this world-wide regeneration." . . . . "By the righteousness of the one true God! If one speck of a jewel be lost and buried beneath a mountain of stones, and lie hidden beyond the seven seas, the Hand of Omnipotence would assuredly reveal it in this Day, pure and cleansed from dross."

Bahá'u'lláh, *The Advent of Divine Justice*, p. 67

October 15

FEAST OF KNOWLEDGE

It is Our wish and desire that every one of you may become a source of all goodness unto men, and an example of uprightness to mankind. Beware lest ye prefer yourselves above your neighbours. Fix your gaze upon Him Who is the Temple of God amongst men. He, in truth, hath offered up His life as a ransom for the redemption of the world. He, verily, is the All-Bountiful, the Gracious, the Most High. If any differences arise amongst you, behold Me standing before your face, and overlook the faults of one another for My name's sake and as a token of your love for My manifest and resplendent Cause.

Bahá'u'lláh, *Gleanings from the Writings of Bahá'u'lláh*, p. 315

THE MONTH OF KNOWLEDGE
BEGINS AT SUNSET

October 16

O SON OF BEING!
Thy heart is My home; sanctify it for My descent. Thy spirit is My place of revelation; cleanse it for My manifestation.

Bahá'u'lláh, *The Hidden Words of Bahá'u'lláh*, No. 59 (Arabic)

October 17

Consider the pettiness of men's minds. They ask for that which injureth them, and cast away the thing that profiteth them. They are, indeed, of those that are far astray. We find some men desiring liberty, and priding themselves therein. Such men are in the depths of ignorance.

Liberty must, in the end, lead to sedition, whose flames none can quench. Thus warneth you He Who is the Reckoner, the All-Knowing. Know ye that the embodiment of liberty and its symbol is the animal. That which beseemeth man is submission unto such restraints as will protect him from his own ignorance, and guard him against the harm of the mischief-maker. Liberty causeth man to overstep the bounds of propriety, and to infringe on the dignity of his station. It debaseth him to the level of extreme depravity and wickedness.

Regard men as a flock of sheep that need a shepherd for their protection. This, verily, is the truth, the certain truth.

Bahá'u'lláh, *Gleanings from the Writings of Bahá'u'lláh*, pp. 335-336

October 18

True liberty consisteth in man's submission unto My commandments, little as ye know it. Were men to observe that which We have sent down unto them from the Heaven of Revelation, they would, of a certainty, attain unto perfect liberty. Happy is the man that hath apprehended the Purpose of God in whatever He hath revealed from the Heaven of His Will, that pervadeth all created things. Say: The liberty that profiteth you is to be found nowhere except in complete servitude unto God, the Eternal Truth. Whoso hath tasted of its sweetness will refuse to barter it for all the dominion of earth and heaven.

Bahá'u'lláh, *Gleanings from the Writings of Bahá'u'lláh*, p. 336

October 19

The Ancient Beauty hath consented to be bound with chains that mankind may be released from its bondage, and hath accepted to be made a prisoner within this most mighty Stronghold that the whole world may attain unto true liberty. He hath drained to its dregs the cup of sorrow, that all the peoples of the earth may attain unto abiding joy and be filled with gladness. This is of the mercy of your Lord, the Compassionate, the Most Merciful. We have accepted to be abased, O believers in the Unity of God, that ye may be exalted, and have suffered manifold afflictions, that ye might prosper and flourish.

Bahá'u'lláh, *Gleanings from the Writings of Bahá'u'lláh*, pp. 99-100

THE ANNIVERSARY OF THE BIRTH OF THE BAB BEGINS AT SUNSET

October 20

I am the Primal Point from which have been generated all created things . . . I am the Countenance of God Whose splendour can never be obscured, the light of God whose radiance can never fade . . . All the keys of heaven God hath chosen to place on My right hand, and all the keys of hell on My left . . . I am one of the sustaining pillars of the Primal Word of God. Whosoever hath recognized Me, hath known all that is true and right, and hath attained all that is good and seemly . . . The substance wherewith God hath created Me is not the clay out of which others have been formed. He hath conferred upon Me that which the worldly-wise can never comprehend, nor the faithful discover.

The Báb, *The World Order of Bahá'u'lláh*, p. 126

October 21

"God the true One is My Witness! This is the Day whereon it is incumbent upon every one that seeth to behold, and every ear that hearkeneth to hear, and every heart that understandeth to perceive, and every tongue that speaketh to proclaim unto all who are in heaven and on earth, this holy, this exalted, and all-highest Name." "Say, O men! This is a matchless Day. Matchless must, likewise, be the tongue that celebrateth the praise of the Desire of all nations, and matchless the deed that aspireth to be acceptable in His sight. The whole human race hath longed for this Day, that perchance it may fulfill that which well beseemeth its station and is worthy of its destiny."

Bahá'u'lláh, *The Advent of Divine Justice*, pp. 66-67

October 22

Say: O people! Withhold not from yourselves the grace of God and His mercy. Whoso withholdeth himself therefrom is indeed in grievous loss. . . . He it is Who hath created you; He it is Who hath nourished your souls through His Cause, and enabled you to recognize Him Who is the Almighty, the Most Exalted, the All-Knowing. . . . Judge ye fairly the Cause of God, your Creator, and behold that which hath been sent down from the Throne on high, and meditate thereon with innocent and sanctified hearts. Then will the truth of this Cause appear unto you as manifest as the sun in its noon-tide glory. Then will ye be of them that have believed in Him.

Bahá'u'lláh, *Gleanings from the Writings of Bahá'u'lláh*, pp. 104-105

October 23

The door of the knowledge of the Ancient Being hath ever been, and will continue for ever to be, closed in the face of men. No man's understanding shall ever gain access unto His holy court. As a token of His mercy, however, and as a proof of His loving-kindness, He hath manifested unto men the Day Stars of His divine guidance, the Symbols of His divine unity, and hath ordained the knowledge of these sanctified Beings to be identical with the knowledge of His own Self. Whoso recognizeth them hath recognized God. Whoso hearkeneth to their call, hath hearkened to the Voice of God, and whoso testifieth to the truth of their Revelation, hath testified to the truth of God Himself.

Bahá'u'lláh, *Gleanings from the Writings of Bahá'u'lláh*, pp. 49-50

October 24

"By the sorrows which afflict the beauty of the All-Glorious! Such is the station ordained for the true believer that if to an extent smaller than a needle's eye the glory of that station were to be unveiled to mankind, every beholder would be consumed away in his longing to attain it. For this reason it hath been decreed that in this earthly life the full measure of the glory of his own station should remain concealed from the eyes of such a believer." "If the veil be lifted, and the full glory of the station of those who have turned wholly towards God, and in their love for Him renounced the world, be made manifest, the entire creation would be dumbfounded."

Bahá'u'lláh, *The Advent of Divine Justice*, p. 64

October 25

And when He desired to manifest grace and beneficence to men, and to set the world in order, He revealed observances and created laws; among them He established the law of marriage, made it as a fortress for well-being and salvation, and enjoined it upon us in that which was sent down out of the heaven of sanctity in His Most Holy Book. He saith, great is His glory: "Marry, O people, that from you may appear he who will remember Me amongst My servants; this is one of My commandments unto you; obey it as an assistance to yourselves."

Bahá'u'lláh, *Bahá'í Prayers*, (U.S. edition 1982), p. 105

October 26

The friends of God must so live and conduct themselves, and evince such excellence of character and conduct, as to make others astonished. The love between husband and wife should not be purely physical, nay rather it must be spiritual and heavenly. These two souls should be considered as one soul. How difficult it would be to divide a single soul! Nay, great would be the difficulty!

In short, the foundation of the Kingdom of God is based upon harmony and love, oneness, relationship and union, not upon differences, especially between husband and wife. If one of these two become the cause of divorce, that one will unquestionably fall into great difficulties, will become the victim of formidable calamities and experience deep remorse.

'Abdu'l-Bahá, *Bahá'í Marriage and Family Life*, p. 9

October 27

God doth verily love union and concord, and abhorreth separation and divorce.

Bahá'u'lláh, *Bahá'í Marriage and Family Life*, p. 8

At all times hath union and association been well-pleasing in the sight of God, and separation and dissension abhorred. Hold fast unto that which God loveth and is His command unto you. He, verily, is the All-Knowing and the All-Seeing, and He is the All-Wise Ordainer.

Bahá'u'lláh, *Bahá'í Marriage and Family Life*, p. 28

October 28

The world of humanity has two wings—one is women and the other men. Not until both wings are equally developed can the bird fly. Should one wing remain weak, flight is impossible. Not until the world of women becomes equal to the world of man in the acquisition of virtues and perfections, can success and prosperity be attained as they ought to be.　　　　　'Abdu'l-Bahá, *Bahá'í Revelation*, p. 212

Divine justice demands that the rights of both sexes should be equally respected since neither is superior to the other in the eyes of Heaven. Dignity before God depends not on sex, but on purity and luminosity of heart. Human virtues belong equally to all!　　　　　'Abdu'l-Bahá, *Paris Talks*, p. 162

October 29

The source of all good is trust in God, submission unto His command, and contentment with His holy will and pleasure.

The essence of wisdom is the fear of God, the dread of His scourge and punishment, and the apprehension of His justice and decree.

The essence of religion is to testify unto that which the Lord hath revealed, and follow that which He hath ordained in His mighty Book.

Bahá'u'lláh, *Tablets of Bahá'u'lláh*, p. 155

October 30

The source of all glory is acceptance of whatso-ever the Lord hath bestowed, and contentment with that which God hath ordained.

The essence of love is for man to turn his heart to the Beloved One, and sever himself from all else but Him, and desire naught save that which is the desire of his Lord.

True remembrance is to make mention of the Lord, the All-Praised, and forget aught else beside Him.

Bahá'u'lláh, *Tablets of Bahá'u'lláh*, p. 155

October 31

O thou who art turning thy face towards God!
Close thine eyes to all things else, and open them to
the realm of the All-Glorious. Ask whatsoever thou
wishest of Him alone; seek whatsoever thou seekest
from Him alone. With a look He granteth a hundred
thousand hopes, with a glance He healeth a hundred
thousand incurable ills, with a glimpse He layeth
balm on every wound, with a nod He freeth the
hearts from the shackles of grief. He doeth as He
doeth, and what recourse have we? He carrieth out
His Will, He ordaineth what He pleaseth. Then
better for thee to bow down thy head in submission,
and put thy trust in the All-Merciful Lord.

'Abdu'l-Bahá, *Selections from the Writings
of 'Abdu'l-Bahá*, p. 51

November 1

O peoples of the earth! God, the Eternal Truth, is My witness that streams of fresh and soft-flowing waters have gushed from the rocks, through the sweetness of the words uttered by your Lord, the Unconstrained; and still ye slumber. Cast away that which ye possess, and, on the wings of detachment, soar beyond all created things. Thus biddeth you the Lord of creation, the movement of Whose Pen hath revolutionized the soul of mankind.

Bahá'u'lláh, *Gleanings from the Writings of Bahá'u'lláh*, p. 139

November 2

There is no paradise, in the estimation of the believers in the Divine Unity, more exalted than to obey God's commandments, and there is no fire in the eyes of those who have known God and His signs, fiercer than to transgress His laws and to oppress another soul, even to the extent of a mustard seed. On the Day of Resurrection God will, in truth, judge all men, and we all verily plead for His grace.

The Báb, *Selections from the Writings of the Báb*, p. 79

November 3

FEAST OF POWER

At these meetings [the Feasts], there should be no extraneous conversation whatever. Rather, the assemblage should confine itself to reading and reciting the Holy Words, and to the discussion of matters relating to the Cause of God, expounding, for example, conclusive proofs and arguments, and the Writings of the Best Beloved of mankind. Those who present themselves at these gatherings must first array themselves in spotless clothing, turn their faces toward the Kingdom of Abhá, and then with lowliness and submissiveness enter in. During the readings they must maintain complete silence. Should anyone wish to speak, he should say his say in all humility, with exactitude and eloquence. Salutations be unto you, and praise.

'Abdu'l-Bahá, *Bahá'í Meetings; The Nineteen Day Feast*, p. 9

THE MONTH OF POWER
BEGINS AT SUNSET

November 4

O SON OF SPIRIT!

The best beloved of all things in My sight is Justice; turn not away therefrom if thou desirest Me, and neglect it not that I may confide in thee. By its aid thou shalt see with thine own eyes and not through the eyes of others, and shalt know of thine own knowledge and not through the knowledge of thy neighbour. Ponder this in thy heart; how it behooveth thee to be. Verily justice is My gift to thee and the sign of My loving-kindness. Set it then before thine eyes.

Bahá'u'lláh, *The Hidden Words of Bahá'u'lláh*,
No. 2 (Arabic)

November 5

Behold how the manifold grace of God, which is being showered from the clouds of Divine glory, hath, in this day, encompassed the world. For whereas in days past every lover besought and searched after his Beloved, it is the Beloved Himself Who now is calling His lovers and is inviting them to attain His presence. Take heed lest ye forfeit so precious a favour; beware lest ye belittle so remarkable a token of His grace. Abandon not the incorruptible benefits, and be not content with that which perisheth. Lift up the veil that obscureth your vision, and dispel the darkness with which it is enveloped, that ye may gaze on the naked beauty of the Beloved's face, may behold that which no eye hath beheld, and hear that which no ear hath heard.

Bahá'u'lláh, *Gleanings from the Writings of Bahá'u'lláh*, p. 320

November 6

How vast the number of people who are well versed in every science, yet it is their adherence to the holy Word of God which will determine their faith, inasmuch as the fruit of every science is none other than the knowledge of divine precepts and submission unto His good-pleasure.

The Báb, *Selections from the Writings of the Báb*, p. 88

The beginning of all things is the knowledge of God, and the end of all things is strict observance of whatsoever hath been sent down from the empyrean of the Divine Will that pervadeth all that is in the heavens and all that is on the earth.

Bahá'u'lláh, *Gleanings from the Writings of Bahá'u'lláh*, p. 5

November 7

As to the difference between that material civilization now prevailing, and the divine civilization which will be one of the benefits to derive from the House of Justice, it is this: material civilization, through the power of punitive and retaliatory laws, restraineth the people from criminal acts; and notwithstanding this, while laws to retaliate against and punish a man are continually proliferating, as ye can see, no laws exist to reward him. In all the cities of Europe and America, vast buildings have been erected to serve as jails for the criminals.

Divine civilization, however, so traineth every member of society that no one, with the exception of a negligible few, will undertake to commit a crime. There is thus a great difference between the prevention of crime through measures that are violent and retaliatory, and so training the people, and enlightening them, and spiritualizing them, that without any fear of punishment or vengeance to come, they will shun all criminal acts. They will, indeed, look upon the very commission of a crime as a great disgrace and in itself the harshest of punishments. They will become enamoured of human perfections, and will consecrate their lives to whatever will bring light to the world and will further those qualities which are acceptable at the Holy Threshold of God.

'Abdu'l-Bahá, *Selections from the Writings*
of 'Abdu'l-Bahá, pp. 132-133

November 8

See then how wide is the difference between material civilization and divine. With force and punishments, material civilization seeketh to restrain the people from mischief, from inflicting harm on society and committing crimes. But in a divine civilization, the individual is so conditioned that with no fear of punishment, he shunneth the perpetration of crimes, seeth the crime itself as the severest of torments, and with alacrity and joy, setteth himself to acquiring the virtues of humankind, to furthering human progress, and to spreading light across the world.

'Abdu'l-Bahá, *Selections from the Writings of 'Abdu'l-Bahá*, p. 133

November 9

True reliance is for the servant to pursue his profession and calling in this world, to hold fast unto the Lord, to seek naught but His grace, inasmuch as in His Hands is the destiny of all His servants.

The essence of detachment is for man to turn his face towards the courts of the Lord, to enter His Presence, behold His Countenance, and stand as witness before Him.

The essence of understanding is to testify to one's poverty, and submit to the Will of the Lord, the Sovereign, the Gracious, the All-Powerful.

The source of courage and power is the promotion of the Word of God, and steadfastness in His Love.   Bahá'u'lláh, *Tablets of Bahá'u'lláh*, pp. 155-156

November 10

The essence of charity is for the servant to recount the blessings of His Lord, and to render thanks unto Him at all times and under all conditions.

The essence of faith is fewness of words and abundance of deeds; he whose words exceed his deeds, know verily his death is better than his life.

The essence of true safety is to observe silence, to look at the end of things and to renounce the world.
Bahá'u'lláh, *Tablets of Bahá'u'lláh*, p. 156

November 11

The beginning of magnanimity is when man expendeth his wealth on himself, on his family and on the poor among his brethren in his Faith.

The essence of wealth is love for Me; whoso loveth Me is the possessor of all things, and he that loveth Me not is indeed of the poor and needy. This is that which the Finger of Glory and Splendour hath revealed. Bahá'u'lláh, *Tablets of Bahá'u'lláh*, p. 156

November 12

Of all the tributes I have paid to Him Who is to come after Me, the greatest is this, My written confession, that no words of Mine can adequately describe Him, nor can any reference to Him in My Book, the Bayán, do justice to His Cause.

The Báb, *The World Order of Bahá'u'lláh*, p. 100

The Flower, thus far hidden from the sight of men, is unveiled to your eyes. In the open radiance of His glory He standeth before you. His voice summoneth all the holy and sanctified beings to come and be united with Him. Happy is he that turneth thereunto; well is it with him that hath attained, and gazed on the light of so wondrous a countenance.

Bahá'u'lláh, *Gleanings from the Writings of Bahá'u'lláh*, p. 322

November 13

Know ye from what heights your Lord, the All-Glorious is calling? Think ye that ye have recognized the Pen wherewith your Lord, the Lord of all names, commandeth you? Nay, by My life! Did ye but know it, ye would renounce the world, and would hasten with your whole hearts to the presence of the Well-Beloved. Your spirits would be so transported by His Word as to throw into commotion the Greater World—how much more this small and petty one! Thus have the showers of My bounty been poured down from the heaven of My loving-kindness, as a token of My grace; that ye may be of the thankful.

Bahá'u'lláh, *Gleanings from the Writings of Bahá'u'lláh*, pp. 139-140

November 14

Night hath succeeded day, and day hath succeeded night, and the hours and moments of your lives have come and gone, and yet none of you hath, for one instant, consented to detach himself from that which perisheth. Bestir yourselves, that the brief moments that are still yours may not be dissipated and lost.

Bahá'u'lláh, *Gleanings from the Writings of Bahá'u'lláh*, p. 321

November 15

Tear asunder, in My Name, the veils that have grievously blinded your vision, and, through the power born of your belief in the unity of God, scatter the idols of vain imitation. Enter, then, the holy paradise of the good-pleasure of the All-Merciful. Sanctify your souls from whatsoever is not of God, and taste ye the sweetness of rest within the pale of His vast and mighty Revelation, and beneath the shadow of His supreme and infallible authority. Suffer not yourselves to be wrapt in the dense veils of your selfish desires, inasmuch as I have perfected in every one of you My creation, so that the excellence of My handiwork may be fully revealed unto men. It follows, therefore, that every man hath been, and will continue to be, able of himself to appreciate the Beauty of God, the Glorified. Had he not been endowed with such a capacity, how could he be called to account for his failure?

Bahá'u'lláh, *Gleanings from the Writings
of Bahá'u'lláh*, p. 143

November 16

Leaders of religion in every age have hindered their people from attaining the shores of eternal salvation, inasmuch as they held the reins of authority in their mighty grasp. Some for the lust of leadership, others through want of knowledge and understanding, have been the cause of the deprivation of the people. By their sanction and authority, every Prophet of God hath drunk from the chalice of sacrifice, and winged His flight unto the heights of glory. What unspeakable cruelties they that have occupied the seats of authority and learning have inflicted upon the true Monarchs of the world, those Gems of Divine virtue! Content with a transitory dominion, they have deprived themselves of an everlasting sovereignty. Bahá'u'lláh, *Kitáb-i-Íqán*, p. 15

November 17

Warn, O Salmán, the beloved of the one true God, not to view with too critical an eye the sayings and writings of men. Let them rather approach such sayings and writings in a spirit of open-mindedness and loving sympathy. Those men, however, who, in this Day, have been led to assail, in their inflammatory writings, the tenets of the Cause of God, are to be treated differently. It is incumbent upon all men, each according to his ability, to refute the arguments of those that have attacked the Faith of God. . . . By the righteousness of Him Who, in this Day, crieth within the inmost heart of all created things: ,"God, there is none other God besides Me!" If any man were to arise to defend, in his writings, the Cause of God against its assailants, such a man, however inconsiderable his share, shall be so honoured in the world to come that the Concourse on high would envy his glory. Bahá'u'lláh, *Gleanings from the Writings of Bahá'u'lláh*, pp. 329-330

November 18

When the friends do not endeavour to spread the message, they fail to remember God befittingly, and will not witness the tokens of assistance and confirmation from the Abha Kingdom nor comprehend the divine mysteries. However, when the tongue of the teacher is engaged in teaching, he will naturally himself be stimulated, will become a magnet attracting the divine aid and bounty of the Kingdom, and will be like unto the bird at the hour of dawn, which itself becometh exhilarated by its own singing, its warbling and its melody.

'Abdu'l-Bahá, *The Individual and Teaching: Raising the Divine Call*, p. 10

November 19

Wert thou to open the heart of a single soul by helping him to embrace the Cause of Him Whom God shall make manifest, thine inmost being would be filled with the inspirations of that august Name. It devolveth upon you, therefore, to perform this task in the Days of Resurrection, inasmuch as most people are helpless, and wert thou to open their hearts and dispel their doubts, they would gain admittance into the Faith of God. Therefore, manifest thou this attribute to the utmost of thine ability in the days of Him Whom God shall make manifest. For indeed if thou dost open the heart of a person for His sake, better will it be for thee than every virtuous deed; since deeds are secondary to faith in Him and certitude in His Reality.

The Báb, *Selections from the Writings of the Báb*, p. 133

November 20

The teacher, when teaching, must be himself fully enkindled, so that his utterance, like unto a flame of fire, may exert influence and consume the veil of self and passion. He must also be utterly humble and lowly so that others may be edified, and be totally self-effaced and evanescent so that he may teach with the melody of the Concourse on high——otherwise his teaching will have no effect.

'Abdu'l-Bahá, *Selections from the Writings of 'Abdu'l-Bahá*, p. 270

November 21

Say: The first and foremost testimony establishing His truth is His own Self. Next to this testimony is His Revelation. For whoso faileth to recognize either the one or the other He hath established the words He hath revealed as proof of His reality and truth. This is, verily, an evidence of His tender mercy unto men. He hath endowed every soul with the capacity to recognize the signs of God. How could He, otherwise, have fulfilled His testimony unto men, if ye be of them that ponder His Cause in their hearts. He will never deal unjustly with any one, neither will He task a soul beyond its power. He, verily, is the Compassionate, the All-Merciful.

Bahá'u'lláh, *Gleanings from the Writings of Bahá'u'lláh*, pp. 105-106

November 22

FEAST OF SPEECH

O ye lovers of this wronged one! Cleanse ye your eyes, so that ye behold no man as different from yourselves. See ye no strangers; rather see all men as friends, for love and unity come hard when ye fix your gaze on otherness. And in this new and wondrous age, the Holy Writings say that we must be at one with every people; that we must see neither harshness nor injustice, neither malevolence, nor hostility, nor hate, but rather turn our eyes toward the heaven of ancient glory. For each of the creatures is a sign of God, and it was by the grace of the Lord and His power that each did step into the world; therefore they are not strangers, but in the family; not aliens, but friends, and to be treated as such.

'Abdu'l-Bahá, *Selections from the Writings of 'Abdu'l-Bahá*, p. 24

November 23

O SON OF EARTH!

Wouldst thou have Me, seek none other than Me; and wouldst thou gaze upon My beauty, close thine eyes to the world and all that is therein; for My will and the will of another than Me, even as fire and water, cannot dwell together in one heart.

Bahá'u'lláh, *The Hidden Words of Bahá'u'lláh*,
No. 31 (Arabic)

November 24

The prayerful condition is the best of all conditions, for man in such a state communeth with God, especially when prayer is offered in private and at times when one's mind is free, such as at midnight. Indeed, prayer imparteth life.

'Abdu'l-Bahá, *Spiritual Foundations: Prayer, Meditation and the Devotional Attitude*, p. 8

November 25

The reason why privacy hath been enjoined in moments of devotion is this, that thou mayest give thy best attention to the remembrance of God, that thy heart may at all times be animated with His Spirit, and not be shut out as by a veil from thy Best Beloved. Let not thy tongue pay lip service in praise of God while thy heart be not attuned to the exalted Summit of Glory, and the Focal Point of communion. Thus if haply thou dost live in the Day of Resurrection, the mirror of thy heart will be set towards Him Who is the Day-Star of Truth; and no sooner will His light shine forth than the splendour thereof shall forthwith be reflected in thy heart.

The Báb, *Selections from the Writings of the Báb*, pp. 93-94

THE ANNIVERSARY OF THE DAY OF THE COVENANT
BEGINS AT SUNSET

November 26

Consider that which We have revealed in Our Most Holy Book: "When the ocean of My presence hath ebbed and the Book of My Revelation is ended, turn your faces toward Him Whom God hath purposed, Who hath branched from this Ancient Root." The object of this sacred verse is none other except the Most Mighty Branch ('Abdu'l-Bahá). Thus have We graciously revealed unto you our potent Will, and I am verily the Gracious, the All-Powerful.

Bahá'u'lláh, *World Order of Bahá'u'lláh*, p. 134

Were it not for the protecting power of the Covenant to guard the impregnable fort of the Cause of God, there would arise among the Bahá'ís, in one day, a thousand different sects as was the case in former ages. 'Abdu'l-Bahá, *Bahá'í World Faith*, pp. 357-358

November 27

Today, no soul has any station or enjoys any title except the soul who is firm in the Covenant and steadfast in the Testament, who entirely forgets himself and is released from the world.

Firmness in the Covenant means obedience, so that no one may say this is my opinion. Nay rather, he must obey that which proceeds from the pen and tongue of the Covenant.

As thou hast realized thy own shortcomings, rest thou assured that thou art firm in the Covenant and Testament, and in the love of the True One art steadfast and growing.

'Abdu'l-Bahá, *Star of the West*, Vol. VIII, pp. 217, 218, 228

THE ANNIVERSARY OF THE ASCENSION OF 'ABDÚ'L-BAHÁ BEGINS AT SUNSET. IT SHOULD BE COMMEMORATED AT 1:00 A.M. ON NOVEMBER 28

November 28

There hath branched from the Sadratu'l-Muntahá this sacred and glorious Being, this Branch of Holiness; well is it with him that hath sought His shelter and abideth beneath His shadow.... Render thanks unto God, O people, for His appearance; for verily He is the most great Favour unto you, the most perfect bounty upon you; and through Him every mouldering bone is quickened. Whoso turneth towards Him hath turned towards God, and whoso turneth away from Him hath turned away from My Beauty, hath repudiated My Proof, and transgressed against Me. He is the Trust of God amongst you, His charge within you, His manifestation unto you and His appearance among His favoured servants . . .

Bahá'u'lláh, *The World Order of Bahá'u'lláh*, p. 135

Fear not, fear not if this Branch be severed from this material world and cast aside its leaves; nay, the leaves thereof shall flourish, for this Branch will grow after it is cut off from this world below, it shall reach the loftiest pinnacles of glory, and it shall bear such fruits as will perfume the world with their fragrance.

'Abdu'l-Bahá, *The World Order of Bahá'u'lláh*, p. 146

November 29

Unto the Most Holy Book every one must turn and all that is not expressly recorded therein must be referred to the Universal House of Justice. That which this body, whether unanimously or by a majority doth carry, that is verily the Truth and the Purpose of God Himself. Whoso doth deviate therefrom is verily of them that love discord, hath shown forth malice and turned away from the Lord of the Covenant. By this House is meant that Universal House of Justice which is to be elected from all countries, that is, from those parts in the East and West where the loved ones are to be found after the manner of the customary elections in Western countries such as those of England.

It is incumbent upon these members (of the Universal House of Justice) to gather in a certain place and deliberate upon all problems which have caused difference, questions that are obscure and matters that are not expressly recorded in the Book. Whatsoever they decide has the same effect as the Text itself. And inasmuch as this House of Justice hath power to enact laws that are not expressly recorded in the Book and bear upon daily transactions, so also it hath power to repeal the same. . . . This it can do because that law formeth no part of the Divine Explicit Text. The House of Justice is both the Initiator and the Abrogator of its own laws.

'Abdu'l-Bahá, *Bahá'í World Faith*, pp. 447-448

November 30

. . . one of the greatest and most fundamental principles of the Cause of God is to shun and avoid entirely the Covenant-breakers, for they will utterly destroy the Cause of God, exterminate His Law and render of no account all efforts exerted in the past. O friends! It behoveth you to call to mind with tenderness the trials of His Holiness, the Exalted One and show your fidelity to the Ever-Blest Beauty. The utmost endeavour must be exerted lest all these woes, trials and afflictions, all this pure and sacred blood that hath been shed so profusely in the Path of God, may prove to be in vain.

O ye beloved of the Lord! Strive with all your heart to shield the Cause of God from the onslaught of the insincere, for souls such as these cause the straight to become crooked and all benevolent efforts to produce contrary results.

'Abdu'l-Bahá, *Bahá'í World Faith*, p. 448

December 1

"Say: no man can attain his true station except through his justice. No power can exist except through unity. No welfare and no well-being can be attained except through consultation."

"Consultation bestoweth greater awareness and transmuteth conjecture into certitude. It is a shining light which, in a dark world, leadeth the way and guideth. For everything there is and will continue to be a station of perfection and maturity. The maturity of the gift of understanding is made manifest through consultation."

Bahá'u'lláh, *Consultation: A Compilation*, p. 3

December 2

If they agree upon a subject, even though it be wrong, it is better than to disagree and be in the right, for this difference will produce the demolition of the divine foundation. Though one of the parties may be in the right and they disagree that will be the cause of a thousand wrongs, but if they agree and both parties are in the wrong, as it is in unity the truth will be revealed and the wrong made right.

'Abdu'l-Bahá, *Bahá'í World Faith*, p. 411

December 3

In the contingent world there are many collective centres which are conducive to association and unity between the children of men. . . . and the prosperity of the world of humanity is dependent upon the organization and promotion of the collective centres. Nevertheless, all the above institutions are, in reality, the matter and not the substance, . . . With the appearance of great revolutions and upheavals, all these collective centres are swept away. But the Collective Centre of the Kingdom, embodying the Institutes and Divine Teachings, is the eternal Collective Centre. It establishes relationship between the East and the West, organizes the oneness of the world of humanity, and destroys the foundation of differences.

'Abdu'l-Bahá, *Tablets of the Divine Plan*, pp. 93-94

December 4

What mankind needeth in this day is obedience unto them that are in authority, and a faithful adherence to the cord of wisdom. The instruments which are essential to the immediate protection, the security and assurance of the human race have been entrusted to the hands, and lie in the grasp, of the governors of human society. This is the wish of God and His decree. Bahá'u'lláh, *Gleanings from the Writings of Bahá'u'lláh*, p. 207

The law must reign and not the individual; thus will the world become a place of beauty and true brotherhood will be realized.

'Abdu'l-Bahá, *Paris Talks*, p. 132

December 5

And now concerning thy question regarding the soul of man and its survival after death. Know thou of a truth that the soul, after its separation from the body, will continue to progress until it attaineth the presence of God, in a state and condition which neither the revolution of ages and centuries, nor the changes and chances of this world, can alter. It will endure as long as the Kingdom of God, His sovereignty, His dominion and power will endure. It will manifest the signs of God and His attributes, and will reveal His loving kindness and bounty.

Bahá'u'lláh, *Gleanings from the Writings of Bahá'u'lláh*, pp. 155-156

December 6

   The honour with which the Hand of Mercy will invest the soul is such as no tongue can adequately reveal, nor any other earthly agency describe. Blessed is the soul which, at the hour of its separation from the body, is sanctified from the vain imaginings of the peoples of the world. Such a soul liveth and moveth in accordance with the Will of its Creator, and entereth the all-highest Paradise.

Bahá'u'lláh, *Gleanings from the Writings of Bahá'u'lláh*, p. 156

December 7

The nature of the soul after death can never be described, nor is it meet and permissible to reveal its whole character to the eyes of men. The Prophets and Messengers of God have been sent down for the sole purpose of guiding mankind to the straight Path of Truth. The purpose underlying their revelation hath been to educate all men, that they may, at the hour of death, ascend, in the utmost purity and sanctity and with absolute detachment, to the throne of the Most High. The light which these souls radiate is responsible for the progress of the world and the advancement of its peoples.

Bahá'u'lláh, *Gleanings from the Writings of Bahá'u'lláh*, pp. 156-157

December 8

True death is realized when a person dieth to himself at the time of His Revelation in such wise that he seeketh naught except Him.

True resurrection from the sepulchres means to be quickened in conformity with His Will, through the power of His utterance.

Paradise is attainment of His good-pleasure and everlasting hell-fire His judgement through justice.

The Day He revealeth Himself is Resurrection Day which shall last as long as He ordaineth.

Everything belongeth unto Him and is fashioned by Him. All besides Him are His creatures.

The Báb, *Selections from the Writings of the Báb*, pp. 157-158

December 9

Do thou beseech God to enable thee to remain steadfast in this path, and to aid thee to guide the peoples of the world to Him Who is the manifest and sovereign Ruler, Who hath revealed Himself in a distinct attire, Who giveth utterance to a Divine and specific Message. This is the essence of faith and certitude. They that are the worshipers of the idol which their imaginations have carved, and who call it Inner Reality, such men are in truth accounted among the heathen. To this hath the All-Merciful borne witness in His Tablets. He, verily, is the All-Knowing, the All-Wise.

Bahá'u'lláh, *Gleanings from the Writings
of Bahá'u'lláh*, p. 338

December 10

O My servants! Could ye apprehend with what wonders of My munificence and bounty I have willed to entrust your souls, ye would, of a truth, rid yourselves of attachment to all created things, and would gain a true knowledge of your own selves—a knowledge which is the same as the comprehension of Mine own Being. Ye would find yourselves independent of all else but Me, and would perceive, with your inner and outer eye, and as manifest as the revelation of My effulgent Name, the seas of My loving-kindness and bounty moving within you.

Bahá'u'lláh, *Bahá'í World Faith*, p. 67

December 11

This Feast was established by His Highness the Báb, to occur once in nineteen days. Likewise, the Blessed Perfection (Bahá'u'lláh) hath commanded, encouraged and reiterated it. Therefore, it hath the utmost importance. Undoubtedly you must give the greatest attention to its establishment and raise it to the highest point of importance, so that it may become continual and constant. . . . The owner of the house must personally serve the beloved ones. He must seek after the comfort of all and with the utmost humility he must show forth kindness to every one.
'Abdu'l-Bahá, *Bahá'í Meetings; The Nineteen Day Feast*, pp. 19-20

December 12

O BEFRIENDED STRANGER!
The candle of thine heart is lighted by the hand of My power, quench it not with the contrary winds of self and passion. The healer of all thine ills is remembrance of Me, forget it not. Make My love thy treasure and cherish it even as thy very sight and life.   Bahá'u'lláh, *The Hidden Words of Bahá'u'lláh*,
No. 32 (Persian)

December 13

By My life! Neither the pomp of the mighty, nor the wealth of the rich, nor even the ascendancy of the ungodly will endure. All will perish, at a word from Him. He, verily, is the All-Powerful, the All-Compelling, the Almighty. What advantage is there in the earthly things which men possess? That which shall profit them, they have utterly neglected. Erelong, they will awake from their slumber, and find themselves unable to obtain that which hath escaped them in the days of their Lord, the Almighty, the All-Praised. Did they but know it, they would renounce their all, that their names may be mentioned before His throne. They, verily, are accounted among the dead.

Bahá'u'lláh, *Gleanings from the Writings of Bahá'u'lláh*, pp. 138-139

December 14

Should a man wish to adorn himself with the ornaments of the earth, to wear its apparels, or partake of the benefits it can bestow, no harm can befall him, if he alloweth nothing whatever to intervene between him and God, for God hath ordained every good thing, whether created in the heavens or in the earth, for such of His servants as truly believe in Him. Eat ye, O people, of the good things which God hath allowed you, and deprive not yourselves from His wondrous bounties. Render thanks and praise unto Him, and be of them that are truly thankful. Bahá'u'lláh, *Gleanings from the Writings of Bahá'u'lláh*, p. 276

December 15

Be not grieved if affairs become difficult and troubles wax intense on all sides! Verily, thy Lord changeth hardship into facility, troubles into ease and afflictions into greatest composure.

If thy daily living become difficult, soon (God) thy Lord will bestow upon thee that which will satisfy thee. Be patient in the time of affliction and trial, endure every difficulty and hardship with a dilated heart, attracted spirit and eloquent tongue in remembrance of the Merciful. Verily this is the life of satisfaction, the spiritual existence, heavenly repose, divine benediction and the celestial table! Soon thy Lord will extenuate thy straitened circumstances even in this world.

'Abdu'l-Bahá, *The Divine Art of Living*, p. 93

December 16

The mind and spirit of man advance when he is tried by suffering. . . . Just as the plow furrows the earth deeply, purifying it of weeds and thistles, so suffering and tribulation free man from the petty affairs of this worldly life until he arrives at a state of complete detachment. His attitude in this world will be that of divine happiness. Man is, so to speak, unripe: the heat of the fire of suffering will mature him. Look back to the times past and you will find that the greatest men have suffered most. . . .

Through suffering he [man] will attain to an eternal happiness which nothing can take from him. . . .

To attain eternal happiness one must suffer. He who has reached the state of self-sacrifice has true joy. Temporal joy will vanish.

'Abdu'l-Bahá, *Paris Talks*, pp. 178-179

December 17

Hear Me, ye mortal birds! In the Rose Garden of changeless splendour a Flower hath begun to bloom, compared to which every other flower is but a thorn, and before the brightness of Whose glory the very essence of beauty must pale and wither. Arise, therefore, and, with the whole enthusiasm of your hearts, with all the eagerness of your souls, the full fervour of your will, and the concentrated efforts of your entire being, strive to attain the paradise of His presence, and endeavour to inhale the fragrance of the incorruptible Flower, to breathe the sweet savours of holiness, and to obtain a portion of this perfume of celestial glory. Whoso followeth this counsel will break his chains asunder, will taste the abandonment of enraptured love, will attain unto his heart's desire, and will surrender his soul into the hands of his Beloved. Bursting through his cage, he will, even as the bird of the spirit, wing his flight to his holy and everlasting nest.

Bahá'u'lláh, *Gleanings from the Writings of Bahá'u'lláh*, pp. 320-321

December 18

Whatever is in the heavens and whatever is on the earth is a direct evidence of the revelation within it of the attributes and names of God, inasmuch as within every atom are enshrined the signs that bear eloquent testimony to the revelation of that Most Great Light. Methinks, but for the potency of that revelation, no being could ever exist. How resplendent the luminaries of knowledge that shine in an atom, and how vast the oceans of wisdom that surge within a drop! To a supreme degree is this true of man, who, among all created things, hath been invested with the robe of such gifts, and hath been singled out for the glory of such distinction. For in him are potentially revealed all the attributes and names of God to a degree that no other created being hath excelled or surpassed.

Bahá'u'lláh, *Gleanings from the Writings of Bahá'u'lláh*, p. 177

December 19

    . . . all things, in their inmost reality, testify to the revelation of the names and attributes of God within them. Each according to its capacity, indicateth, and is expressive of, the knowledge of God. So potent and universal is this revelation, that it hath encompassed all things visible and invisible. . . . Man, the noblest and most perfect of all created things, excelleth them all in the intensity of this revelation, and is a fuller expression of its glory. And of all men, the most accomplished, the most distinguished, and the most excellent are the Manifestations of the Sun of Truth. Nay, all else besides these Manifestations, live by the operation of their Will, and move and have their being through the outpourings of their grace.

Bahá'u'lláh, *Gleanings from the Writings*
of Bahá'u'lláh, pp. 178-179

December 20

"In all matters moderation is desirable. If a thing is carried to excess, it will prove a source of evil. Consider the civilization of the West, how it hath agitated and alarmed the peoples of the world. An infernal engine hath been devised, and hath proved so cruel a weapon of destruction that its like none hath ever witnessed or heard. The purging of such deeply-rooted and overwhelming corruptions cannot be effected unless the peoples of the world unite in pursuit of one common aim and embrace one universal faith. Incline your ears unto the Call of this Wronged One and adhere firmly to the Lesser Peace.

Strange and astonishing things exist in the earth but they are hidden from the minds and the understanding of men. These things are capable of changing the whole atmosphere of the earth and their contamination would prove lethal."

Bahá'u'lláh, *Tablets of Bahá'u'lláh*, p. 69

December 21

Consider how the human intellect develops and weakens, and may at times come to naught, whereas the soul changeth not. For the mind to manifest itself, the human body must be whole; and a sound mind cannot be but in a sound body, whereas the soul dependeth not upon the body. . . . It is by the aid of such senses as those of sight, hearing, taste, smell and touch, that the mind comprehendeth, whereas, the soul is free from all agencies. The soul as thou observest, whether it be in sleep or waking, is in motion and ever active. Possibly it may, whilst in a dream, unravel an intricate problem, incapable of solution in the waking state. The mind, moreover, understandeth not whilst the senses have ceased to function, and in the embryonic stage and in early infancy the reasoning power is totally absent, whereas the soul is ever endowed with full strength.

'Abdu'l-Bahá, *Bahá'í Revelation*, p. 221

December 22

Know thou that all men have been created in the nature made by God, the Guardian, the Self-Subsisting. Unto each one hath been prescribed a pre-ordained measure, as decreed in God's mighty and guarded Tablets. All that which ye potentially possess can, however, be manifested only as a result of your own volition. Your own acts testify to this truth. Consider, for instance, that which hath been forbidden, in the Bayán, unto men. God hath in that Book, and by His behest, decreed as lawful whatsoever He hath pleased to decree, and hath, through the power of His sovereign might, forbidden whatsoever He elected to forbid. . . . Men, however, have wittingly broken His law. Is such a behaviour to be attributed to God, or to their proper selves? Be fair in your judgment. Every good thing is of God, and every evil thing is from yourselves.

Bahá'u'lláh, *Gleanings from the Writings of Bahá'u'lláh*, p. 149

December 23

. . . every man hath been, and will continue to be, able of himself to appreciate the Beauty of God, the Glorified. Had he not been endowed with such a capacity, how could he be called to account for his failure? If, in the Day when all the peoples of the earth will be gathered together, any man should, whilst standing in the presence of God, be asked: "Wherefore hast thou disbelieved in My Beauty and turned away from My Self," and if such a man should reply and say: "Inasmuch as all men have erred, and none hath been found willing to turn his face to the Truth, I, too, following their example, have grievously failed to recognize the Beauty of the Eternal," such a plea will, assuredly, be rejected. For the faith of no man can be conditioned by any one except himself.

Bahá'u'lláh, *Gleanings from the Writings of Bahá'u'lláh*, p. 143

December 24

Oh, would that the world could believe Me! Were all the things that lie enshrined within the heart of Bahá, and which the Lord, His God, the Lord of all names, hath taught Him, to be unveiled to mankind, every man on earth would be dumbfounded.

How great the multitude of truths which the garment of words can never contain! How vast the number of such verities as no expression can adequately describe, whose significance can never be unfolded, and to which not even the remotest allusions can be made! How manifold are the truths which must remain unuttered until the appointed time is come! Even as it hath been said: "Not everything that a man knoweth can be disclosed, nor can everything that he can disclose be regarded as timely, nor can every timely utterance be considered as suited to the capacity of those who hear it."

Bahá'u'lláh, *Gleanings from the Writings of Bahá'u'lláh*, p. 176

December 25

"O friends! Be not careless of the virtues with which ye have been endowed, neither be neglectful of your high destiny. . . . Ye are the stars of the heaven of understanding, the breeze that stirreth at the break of day, the soft-flowing waters upon which must depend the very life of all men, the letters inscribed upon His sacred scroll." "O people of Bahá! Ye are the breezes of spring that are wafted over the world. . . . Beware lest anything withhold you from observing the things prescribed unto you by the Pen of Glory, as it moved over His Tablet with sovereign majesty and might. Great is the blessedness of him that hath hearkened to its shrill voice, as it was raised, through the power of truth, before all who are in heaven and all who are on earth." Bahá'u'lláh, *The Advent of Divine Justice*, pp. 63-64

December 26

While the children are yet in their infancy feed them from the breast of heavenly grace, foster them in the cradle of all excellence, rear them in the embrace of bounty. Give them the advantage of every useful kind of knowledge. Let them share in every new and rare and wondrous craft and art. Bring them up to work and strive, and accustom them to hardship. Teach them to dedicate their lives to matters of great import, and inspire them to undertake studies that will benefit mankind.

'Abdu'l-Bahá, *Selections from the Writings of 'Abdu'l-Bahá*, p. 129

December 27

Let the mothers consider that whatever concerneth the education of children is of the first importance. Let them put forth every effort in this regard, for when the bough is green and tender it will grow in whatever way ye train it. Therefore it is incumbent upon the mothers to rear their little ones even as a gardener tendeth his young plants. Let them strive by day and by night to establish within their children faith and certitude, the fear of God, the love of the Beloved of the worlds, and all good qualities and traits. Whensoever a mother seeth that her child hath done well, let her praise and applaud him and cheer his heart; and if the slightest undesirable trait should manifest itself, let her counsel the child and punish him, and use means based on reason, even a slight verbal chastisement should this be necessary. It is not, however, permissible to strike a child, or vilify him, for the child's character will be totally perverted if he be subjected to blows or verbal abuse.

'Abdu'l-Bahá, *Selections from the Writings of 'Abdu'l-Bahá*, p. 125

December 28

My wish is that these children should receive a Bahá'í education, so that they may progress both here and in the Kingdom, and rejoice thy heart.

In a time to come, morals will degenerate to an extreme degree. It is essential that children be reared in the Bahá'í way, that they may find happiness both in this world and the next. If not, they shall be beset by sorrows and troubles, for human happiness is founded upon spiritual behaviour.

'Abdu'l-Bahá, *Selections from the Writings of 'Abdu'l-Bahá*, p. 127

December 29

Every imperfect soul is self-centred and thinketh only of his own good. But as his thoughts expand a little he will begin to think of the welfare and comfort of his family. If his ideas still more widen, his concern will be the felicity of his fellow citizens; and if they still widen, he will be thinking of the glory of his land and of his race. But when ideas and views reach the utmost degree of expansion and attain the stage of perfection, then will he be interested in the exaltation of humankind. He will then be the well-wisher of all men and the seeker of the weal and prosperity of all lands. This is indicative of perfection.

'Abdu'l-Bahá, *Selections from the Writings
of 'Abdu'l-Bahá*, p. 69

December 30

FEAST OF HONOUR

You have asked as to the Feast in every Bahá'í month. This Feast is held to foster comradeship and love, to call God to mind and supplicate Him with contrite hearts, and to encourage benevolent pursuits.

That is, the friends should there dwell upon God and glorify Him, read the prayers and holy verses, and treat one another with the utmost affection and love.

As to the Nineteen Day Feast, it rejoiceth mind and heart. If this Feast be held in the proper fashion, the friends will, once in nineteen days, find themselves spiritually restored, and endued with a power that is not of this world.

'Abdu'l-Bahá, *Bahá'í Meetings;*
The Nineteen Day Feast, p. 19

THE MONTH OF HONOUR
BEGINS AT SUNSET

December 31

O OFFSPRING OF DUST!

Be not content with the ease of a passing day, and deprive not thyself of everlasting rest. Barter not the garden of eternal delight for the dust-heap of a mortal world. Up from thy prison ascend unto the glorious meads above, and from thy mortal cage wing thy flight unto the paradise of the Placeless.

Bahá'u'lláh, *The Hidden Words of Bahá'u'lláh*,
No. 39 (Persian)

January 1

Until a being setteth his foot in the plane of sacrifice, he is bereft of every favour and grace; and this plane of sacrifice is the realm of dying to the self, that the radiance of the living God may then shine forth. The martyr's field is the place of detachment from self, that the anthems of eternity may be upraised. Do all ye can to become wholly weary of self, and bind yourselves to that Countenance of Splendours; and once ye have reached such heights of servitude, ye will find, gathered within your shadow, all created things. This is boundless grace; this is the highest sovereignty; this is the life that dieth not. All else save this is at the last but manifest perdition and great loss.   'Abdu'l-Bahá, *Selections from the Writings of 'Abdu'l-Bahá*, pp. 76-77

January 2

"God be praised! The sun of justice hath risen above the horizon of Bahá'u'lláh. For in His Tablets the foundations of such a justice have been laid as no mind hath, from the beginning of creation, conceived." "The canopy of existence resteth upon the pole of justice, and not of forgiveness, and the life of mankind dependeth on justice and not on forgiveness."

'Abdu'l-Bahá, *The Advent of Divine Justice*, p. 24

January 3

O ye, God's loved ones! Experience hath shown how greatly the renouncing of smoking, of intoxicating drink, and of opium, conduceth to health and vigour, to the expansion and keenness of the mind and to bodily strength. There is today a people who strictly avoid tobacco, intoxicating liquor and opium. This people is far and away superior to the others, for strength and physical courage, for health, beauty and comeliness. A single one of their men can stand up to ten men of another tribe. This hath proved true of the entire people: that is, member for member, each individual of this community is in every respect superior to the individuals of other communities.

'Abdu'l-Bahá, *Selections from the Writings of 'Abdu'l-Bahá*, p. 150

January 4

Make ye then a mighty effort, that the purity and sanctity which, above all else, are cherished by 'Abdu'l-Bahá, shall distinguish the people of Bahá; that in every kind of excellence the people of God shall surpass all other human beings; that both outwardly and inwardly they shall prove superior to the rest; that for purity, immaculacy, refinement, and the preservation of health, they shall be leaders in the vanguard of those who know. And that by their freedom from enslavement, their knowledge, their self-control, they shall be first among the pure, the free and the wise.

'Abdu'l-Bahá, *Selections from the Writings of 'Abdu'l-Bahá*, p. 150

January 5

In our solar system, the centre of illumination is the sun itself. Through the will of God this central luminary is the one source of the existence and development of all phenomenal things. . . . Without this quickening impulse there would be no growth of tree or vegetation, neither would the existence of animal or human being be possible; in fact no forms of created life would be manifest upon the earth. . . .

Likewise in the spiritual realm of intelligence and idealism there must be a centre of illumination, and that centre is the everlasting, ever-shining Sun, the Word of God. . . . This Sun of Reality, this centre of effulgences is the prophet or Manifestation of God. Just as the phenomenal sun shines upon the material world producing life and growth, likewise the spiritual or prophetic Sun confers illumination upon the human world of thought and intelligence, and unless it rose upon the horizon of human existence the kingdom of man would become dark and extinguished.

'Abdu'l-Bahá, *Bahá'í World Faith*, pp. 254-255

January 6

Just as the earth attracts everything to the centre of gravity, and every object thrown upward into space will come down, so also material ideas and worldly thoughts attract man to the centre of self. Anger, passion, ignorance, prejudice, greed, envy, covetousness, jealousy and suspicion prevent man from ascending to the realms of holiness, imprisoning him in the claws of self and the cage of egotism. The physical man, unassisted by the divine power, trying to escape from one of these invisible enemies, will unconsciously fall into the hands of another. No sooner does he attempt to soar upward than the density of the love of self, like the power of gravity, draws him to the centre of the earth. The only power that is capable of delivering man from this captivity is the power of the breaths of the Holy Spirit. 'Abdu'l-Bahá, *Selections of Bahá'í Scriptures*, p. 241

January 7

It is better to guide one soul than to possess all that is on earth, for as long as that guided soul is under the shadow of the Tree of Divine Unity, he and the one who hath guided him will both be recipients of God's tender mercy, whereas possession of earthly things will cease at the time of death. The path to guidance is one of love and compassion, not of force and coercion. This hath been God's method in the past, and shall continue to be in the future! He causeth him whom He pleaseth to enter the shadow of His Mercy. Verily, He is the Supreme Protector, the All-Generous.

The Báb, *Selections from the Writings of the Báb*, p. 77

January 8

Whoso ariseth to teach Our Cause must needs detach himself from all earthly things, and regard, at all times, the triumph of Our Faith as his supreme objective. This hath, verily, been decreed in the Guarded Tablet. And when he determineth to leave his home, for the sake of the Cause of his Lord, let him put his whole trust in God, as the best provision for his journey, and array himself with the robe of virtue. . . .

If he be kindled with the fire of His love, if he foregoeth all created things, the words he uttereth shall set on fire them that hear him.

Bahá'u'lláh, *Gleanings from the Writings
of Bahá'u'lláh*, pp. 334-335

January 9

If thou wishest to guide the souls, it is incumbent on thee to be firm, to be good and to be imbued with praiseworthy attributes and divine qualities under all circumstances. Be a sign of love, a manifestation of mercy, a fountain of tenderness, kind-hearted, good to all and gentle to the servants of God, and especially to those who bear relation to thee, both men and women. Bear every ordeal that befalleth thee from the people and confront them not save with kindness, with great love and good wishes. 'Abdu'l-Bahá, *The Individual and Teaching: Raising the Divine Call*, p. 10

January 10

Know ye that by "the world" is meant your unawareness of Him Who is your Maker, and your absorption in aught else but Him. The "life to come", on the other hand, signifieth the things that give you a safe approach to God, the All-Glorious, the Incomparable. Whatsoever deterreth you, in this Day, from loving God is nothing but the world. Flee it, that ye may be numbered with the blest.

Bahá'u'lláh, *Gleanings from the Writings of Bahá'u'lláh*, p. 276

January 11

Know verily that the essence of justice and the source thereof are both embodied in the ordinances prescribed by Him who is the Manifestation of the Self of God amongst men, if ye be of them that recognize this truth. He doth verily incarnate the highest, the infallible standard of justice unto all creation. Were His law to be such as to strike terror into the hearts of all that are in heaven and on earth, that law is naught but manifest justice. The fears and agitation which the revelation of this law provokes in men's hearts should indeed be likened to the cries of the suckling babe weaned from his mother's milk, if ye be of them that perceive. Were men to discover the motivating purpose of God's Revelation, they would assuredly cast away their fears, and, with hearts filled with gratitude, rejoice with exceeding gladness.

Bahá'u'lláh, *Gleanings from the Writings of Bahá'u'lláh*, p. 175

January 12

Man is the supreme Talisman. Lack of a proper education hath, however, deprived him of that which he doth inherently possess. Through a word proceeding out of the mouth of God he was called into being; by one word more he was guided to recognize the Source of his education; by yet another word his station and destiny were safeguarded. The Great Being saith: Regard man as a mine rich in gems of inestimable value. Education can, alone, cause it to reveal its treasures, and enable mankind to benefit therefrom. . . . The one true God, exalted be His glory, hath wished nothing for Himself. The allegiance of mankind profiteth Him not, neither doth its perversity harm Him. The Bird of the Realm of Utterance voiceth continually this call: "All things have I willed for thee, and thee, too, for thine own sake."

Bahá'u'lláh, *Gleanings from the Writings of Bahá'u'lláh*, p. 260

January 13

There are two ways of healing sickness, material means and spiritual means. The first is by the treatment of physicians; the second consisteth in prayers offered by the spiritual ones to God and in turning to Him. Both means should be used and practised.

Illnesses which occur by reason of physical causes should be treated by doctors with medical remedies; those which are due to spiritual causes disappear through spiritual means. Thus an illness caused by affliction, fear, nervous impressions, will be healed more effectively by spiritual rather than by physical treatment. Hence, both kinds of treatment should be followed; they are not contradictory.

'Abdu'l-Bahá, *Selections from the Writings of 'Abdu'l-Bahá*, pp. 151-152

January 14

. . . I say unto you that anyone who will rise up in the Cause of God at this time shall be filled with the spirit of God, and that He will send His hosts from heaven to help you, and that nothing shall be impossible to you if you have faith. And now I give you a commandment which shall be for a covenant between you and Me—that ye have faith; that your faith be steadfast as a rock that no storms can move, that nothing can disturb, and that it endure through all things even to the end; even should ye hear that your Lord has been crucified, be not shaken in your faith; for I am with you always, whether living or dead, I am with you to the end. As ye have faith so shall your powers and blessings be. This is the balance—this is the balance—this is the balance.

'Abdu'l-Bahá, *An Early Pilgrimage*, p. 40

January 15

The necessity and the particularity of the assured and believing ones is to be firm in the Cause of God and withstand the hidden and evident tests. Thanks be to God that you are distinguished and made eminent by this blessing. Anybody can be happy in the state of comfort, ease, health, success, pleasure and joy; but if one will be happy and contented in the time of trouble, hardship and prevailing disease, it is the proof of nobility. Thanks be to God that that dear servant of God is extremely patient under the disastrous circumstances, and in the place of complaining gives thanks.

'Abdu'l-Bahá, *Bahá'í World Faith*, pp. 363-364

January 16

Every human creature is the servant of God. All have been created and reared by the power and favour of God; all have been blessed with the bounties of the same Sun of Divine truth; all have quaffed from the fountain of the infinite mercy of God; and all in His estimation and love are equal as servants. He is beneficent and kind to all. Therefore no one should glorify himself over another; no one should manifest pride or superiority toward another; no one should look upon another with scorn and contempt and no one should deprive or oppress a fellow creature. All must be considered as submerged in the ocean of God's mercy. We must associate with all humanity with gentleness and kindliness. We must love all with love of the heart.

'Abdu'l-Bahá, *The Divine Art of Living*, p. 110

January 17

All praise be to God Who hath adorned the world with an ornament, and arrayed it with a vesture, of which it can be despoiled by no earthly power, however mighty its battalions, however vast its wealth, however profound its influence. Say: the essence of all power is God's, the highest and the last End of all creation. The source of all majesty is God's, the Object of the adoration of all that is in the heavens and all that is on the earth. Such forces as have their origin in this world of dust are, by their very nature, unworthy of consideration.

Say: The springs that sustain the life of these birds are not of this world. Their source is far above the reach and ken of human apprehension. Who is there that can put out the light which the snow-white Hand of God hath lit? Where is he to be found that hath the power to quench the fire which hath been kindled through the might of thy Lord, the All-Powerful, the All-Compelling, the Almighty? It is the Hand of Divine might that hath extinguished the flames of dissension. Powerful is He to do that which He pleaseth. He saith: Be; and it is.

Bahá'u'lláh, *Gleanings from the Writings of Bahá'u'lláh*, p. 341

January 18

. . . one of the greatest divine wisdoms regarding the appearance of the Holy Manifestations is this: The souls may come to know each other and become intimate with each other; the power of the love of God may make all of them the waves of one sea, the flowers of one rose garden, and the stars of one heaven. . . .

O ye friends! Fellowship, fellowship! Love, love! Unity, unity!—So that the power of the Bahá'í Cause may appear and become manifest in the world of existence. My thoughts are turned towards you, and my heart leaps within me at your mention. Could ye know how my soul glows with your love, so great a happiness would flood your hearts as to cause you to become enamoured with each other.

'Abdu'l-Bahá, *Tablets of the Divine Plan*, p. 50

THE MONTH OF SOVEREIGNTY
BEGINS AT SUNSET

January 19

O COMPANION OF MY THRONE!

Hear no evil, and see no evil, abase not thyself, neither sigh and weep. Speak no evil, that thou mayest not hear it spoken unto thee, and magnify not the faults of others that thine own faults may not appear great; and wish not the abasement of anyone, that thine own abasement be not exposed. Live then the days of thy life, that are less than a fleeting moment, with thy mind stainless, thy heart unsullied, thy thoughts pure, and thy nature sanctified, so that, free and content, thou mayest put away this mortal frame, and repair unto the mystic paradise and abide in the eternal kingdom for evermore. Bahá'u'lláh, *The Hidden Words of Bahá'u'lláh*, No. 44 (Persian)

January 20

Through the faculty of meditation man attains to eternal life; through it he receives the breath of the Holy Spirit—the bestowal of the Spirit is given in reflection and meditation.

The spirit of man is itself informed and strengthened during meditation; through it affairs of which man knew nothing are unfolded before his view. Through it he receives Divine inspiration, through it he receives heavenly food.

Meditation is the key for opening the doors of mysteries. In that state man abstracts himself: in that state man withdraws himself from all outside objects; in that subjective mood he is immersed in the ocean of spiritual life and can unfold the secrets of things-in-themselves. To illustrate this, think of man as endowed with two kinds of sight; when the power of insight is being used the outward power of vision does not see.   'Abdu'l-Bahá, *Paris Talks*, p. 175

January 21

Know thou that the soul of man is exalted above, and is independent of all infirmities of body or mind. That a sick person showeth signs of weakness is due to the hindrances that interpose themselves between his soul and his body, for the soul itself remaineth unaffected by any bodily ailments. Consider the light of the lamp. Though an external object may interfere with its radiance, the light itself continueth to shine with undiminished power. In like manner, every malady afflicting the body of man is an impediment that preventeth the soul from manifesting its inherent might and power. When it leaveth the body, however, it will evince such ascendancy, and reveal such influence as no force on earth can equal. Every pure, every refined and sanctified soul will be endowed with tremendous power, and shall rejoice with exceeding gladness. Bahá'u'lláh, *Gleanings from the Writings of Bahá'u'lláh*, pp. 153-154

January 22

The reality of man is his thought, not his material body. The thought force and the animal force are partners. Although man is part of the animal creation, he possesses a power of thought superior to all other created beings.

If a man's thought is constantly aspiring towards heavenly subjects then does he become saintly; if on the other hand his thought does not soar, but is directed downwards to centre itself upon the things of this world, he grows more and more material until he arrives at a state little better than that of a mere animal.

'Abdu'l-Bahá, *Paris Talks*, pp. 17-18

January 23

O ye homeless and wanderers in the path of
God! Prosperity, contentment, and freedom,
however much desired and conducive to the
gladness of the human heart, can in no wise compare
with the trials of homelessness and adversity in the
pathway of God; for such exile and banishment are
blessed by the divine favour, and are surely
followed by the mercy of Providence. The joy of
tranquillity in one's home, and the sweetness of
freedom from all cares shall pass away, whilst the
blessing of homelessness shall endure forever, and
its far-reaching results shall be made manifest.

'Abdu'l-Bahá, *Selections from the Writings
of 'Abdu'l-Bahá*, pp. 280-281

January 24

Wherefore are ye downcast and dejected? Why remain despondent when the Pure and Hidden One hath appeared unveiled amongst you? He Who is both the Beginning and the End, He Who is both Stillness and Motion, is now manifest before your eyes. Behold how, in this Day, the Beginning is reflected in the End, how out of Stillness Motion hath been engendered. This motion hath been generated by the potent energies which the words of the Almighty have released throughout the entire creation. Whoso hath been quickened by its vitalizing power, will find himself impelled to attain the court of the Beloved; and whoso hath deprived himself therefrom, will sink into irretrievable despondency. He is truly wise whom the world and all that is therein have not deterred from recognizing the light of this Day, who will not allow men's idle talk to cause him to swerve from the way of righteousness. He is indeed as one dead who, at the wondrous dawn of this Revelation, hath failed to be quickened by its soul-stirring breeze. He is indeed a captive who hath not recognized the Supreme Redeemer, but hath suffered his soul to be bound, distressed and helpless, in the fetters of his desires.

Bahá'u'lláh, *Gleanings from the Writings of Bahá'u'lláh*, pp. 168-169

January 25

Whoso ariseth among you to teach the Cause of his Lord, let him, before all else, teach his own self, that his speech may attract the hearts of them that hear him. Unless he teacheth his own self, the words of his mouth will not influence the heart of the seeker. Take heed, O people, lest ye be of them that give good counsel to others but forget to follow it themselves. The words of such as these, and beyond the words the realities of all things, and beyond these realities the angels that are nigh unto God, bring against them the accusation of falsehood.

Should such a man ever succeed in influencing any one, this success should be attributed not to him, but rather to the influence of the words of God, as decreed by Him Who is the Almighty, the All-Wise. In the sight of God he is regarded as a lamp that imparteth its light, and yet is all the while being consumed within itself.

Bahá'u'lláh, *Gleanings from the Writings of Bahá'u'lláh*, p. 277

January 26

   In every country where any of this people
reside, they must behave towards the government of
that country with loyalty, honesty and truthfulness.
This is that which hath been revealed at the behest of
Him Who is the Ordainer, the Ancient of Days.

Bahá'u'lláh, *Tablets of Bahá'u'lláh*, pp. 22-23

January 27

The Tongue of Grandeur saith: By Myself that speaketh the truth! In this most mighty Revelation all the Dispensations of the past have attained their highest and final consummation. Whoso layeth claim to a Revelation after Him, such a man is assuredly a lying impostor. We pray God that He may graciously assist him to retract and repudiate such claim. Should he repent, God will no doubt forgive him. If, however, he persisteth in his error, God will assuredly send down one who will deal mercilessly with him. He, verily, is the Almighty, the Most Powerful.

Bahá'u'lláh, *Gleanings from the Writings of Bahá'u'lláh*, p. 244

January 28

That one indeed is a man who, today, dedicateth himself to the service of the entire human race. The Great Being saith: Blessed and happy is he that ariseth to promote the best interests of the peoples and kindreds of the earth. In another passage He hath proclaimed: It is not for him to pride himself who loveth his own country, but rather for him who loveth the whole world. The earth is but one country, and mankind its citizens.

Bahá'u'lláh, *The Proclamation of Bahá'u'lláh*, p. 116

January 29

One of the great events which is to occur in the Day of the manifestation of that incomparable Branch is the hoisting of the Standard of God among all nations. By this is meant that all nations and kindreds will be gathered together under the shadow of this Divine Banner, which is no other than the Lordly Branch itself, and will become a single nation. Religious and sectarian antagonism, the hostility of races and peoples, and differences among nations, will be eliminated. All men will adhere to one religion, will have one common faith, will be blended into one race and become a single people. All will dwell in one common fatherland, which is the planet itself.

'Abdu'l-Bahá, *The World Order of Bahá'u'lláh*, pp. 204-205

January 30

The source of all evil is for man to turn away from his Lord and set his heart on things ungodly.

The most burning fire is to question the signs of God, to dispute idly that which He hath revealed, to deny Him and carry one's self proudly before Him.

The source of all learning is the knowledge of God, exalted be His Glory, and this cannot be attained save through the knowledge of His Divine Manifestation. Bahá'u'lláh, *Tablets of Bahá'u'lláh*, p. 156

January 31

The essence of abasement is to pass out from under the shadow of the Merciful and seek the shelter of the Evil One.

The source of error is to disbelieve in the One true God, rely upon aught else but Him, and flee from His Decree.

True loss is for him whose days have been spent in utter ignorance of his self.

The essence of all that We have revealed for thee is Justice, is for man to free himself from idle fancy and imitation, discern with the eye of oneness His glorious handiwork, and look into all things with a searching eye.

Thus have We instructed thee, manifested unto thee Words of Wisdom, that thou mayest be thankful unto the Lord, Thy God, and glory therein amidst all peoples.

Bahá'u'lláh, *Tablets of Bahá'u'lláh*, pp. 156-157

February 1

Release yourselves, O nightingales of God, from the thorns and brambles of wretchedness and misery, and wing your flight to the rose-garden of unfading splendour. O My friends that dwell upon the dust! Haste forth unto your celestial habitation. Announce unto yourselves the joyful tidings: "He Who is the Best-Beloved is come! He hath crowned Himself with the glory of God's Revelation, and hath unlocked to the face of men the doors of His ancient Paradise." Let all eyes rejoice, and let every ear be gladdened, for now is the time to gaze on His beauty, now is the fit time to hearken to His voice. . . . O lovers of His beauty! Turn the anguish of your separation from Him into the joy of an everlasting reunion, and let the sweetness of His presence dissolve the bitterness of your remoteness from His court. Bahá'u'lláh, *Gleanings from the Writings of Bahá'u'lláh*, pp. 319-320

February 2

The advent of the prophets and the revelation of the Holy Books is intended to create love between souls and friendship between the inhabitants of the earth. Real love is impossible unless one turn his face towards God and be attracted to His Beauty.

'Abdu'l-Bahá, *Bahá'í World Faith*, p. 364

February 3

These agitations of the violators are no more than the foam of the ocean, which is one of its inseparable features; but the ocean of the Covenant shall surge and shall cast ashore the bodies of the dead, for it cannot retain them. Thus it is seen that the ocean of the Covenant hath surged and surged until it hath thrown out the dead bodies—souls that are deprived of the Spirit of God and are lost in passion and self and are seeking leadership. This foam of the ocean shall not endure and shall soon disperse and vanish, while the ocean of the Covenant shall eternally surge and roar.

'Abdu'l-Bahá, *Selections from the Writings of 'Abdu'l-Bahá*, pp. 210-211

February 4

Say: O people of the Bayán! We have chosen you out of the world to know and recognize Our Self. We have caused you to draw nigh unto the right side of Paradise—the Spot out of which the undying Fire crieth in manifold accents: "There is none other God besides Me, the All-Powerful, the Most High!" Take heed lest ye allow yourselves to be shut out as by a veil from this Day Star that shineth above the day-spring of the Will of your Lord, the All-Merciful, and whose light hath encompassed both the small and the great. Purge your sight, that ye may perceive its glory with your own eyes, and depend not on the sight of any one except your self, for God hath never burdened any soul beyond its power. Thus hath it been sent down unto the Prophets and Messengers of old, and been recorded in all the Scriptures.

Bahá'u'lláh, *Gleanings from the Writings of Bahá'u'lláh*, pp. 106-107

February 5

An humble man without learning, but filled with the Holy Spirit, is more powerful than the most nobly-born profound scholar without that inspiration.

'Abdu'l-Bahá, *Paris Talks*, p. 165

February 6

FEAST OF DOMINION

We hear that you have in mind to embellish your house from time to time with a meeting of Bahá'ís, where some among them will engage in glorifying the all-glorious Lord. . . . Know that should you bring this about, that house of earth will become a house of Heaven, and that fabric of stone a congress of the spirit.

'Abdu'l-Bahá, *Bahá'í Meetings;
The Nineteen Day Feast*, p. 6

THE MONTH OF DOMINION
BEGINS AT SUNSET

February 7

O HEEDLESS ONES!

Think not the secrets of hearts are hidden, nay, know ye of a certainty that in clear characters they are engraved and are openly manifest in the holy Presence.   Bahá'u'lláh, *The Hidden Words of Bahá'u'lláh,*
No. 59 (Persian)

February 8

The sovereigns of the world must conclude a binding treaty, and establish a covenant, the provisions of which shall be sound, inviolable and definite. They must proclaim it to all the world, and obtain for it the sanction of all the human race . . . All the forces of humanity must be mobilized to insure the stability and permanence of this Most Great Covenant . . . The fundamental principle underlying this solemn Pact should be so fixed that if any government later violate any one of its provisions, all the governments on earth should arise to reduce it to utter submission, nay the human race as a whole should resolve, with every power at its disposal, to destroy that government.

'Abdu'l-Bahá, *World Order of Bahá'u'lláh*, p. 192

February 9

"It is evident that every age in which a Manifestation of God hath lived is divinely-ordained, and may, in a sense, be characterized as God's appointed Day. This Day, however, is unique, and is to be distinguished from those that have preceded it. The designation 'Seal of the Prophets' fully revealeth its high station. The Prophetic Cycle hath verily ended. The Eternal Truth is now come. He hath lifted up the ensign of power, and is now shedding upon the world the unclouded splendour of His Revelation." "In this most mighty Revelation all the Dispensations of the past have attained their highest, their final consummation. That which hath been made manifest in this preeminent, this most exalted Revelation, standeth unparalleled in the annals of the past, nor will future age witness its like."

Bahá'u'lláh, *The World Order of Bahá'u'lláh*, p. 167

February 10

Bahá'u'lláh says there is a sign (from God) in every phenomenon: the sign of the intellect is contemplation and the sign of contemplation is silence, because it is impossible for a man to do two things at one time—he cannot both speak and meditate.

It is an axiomatic fact that while you meditate you are speaking with your own spirit. In that state of mind you put certain questions to your spirit and the spirit answers: the light breaks forth and the reality is revealed.

You cannot apply the name "man" to any being void of this faculty of meditation; without it he would be a mere animal, lower than the beasts.

'Abdu'l-Bahá, *Paris Talks*, pp. 174-175

February 11

The Great Being saith: The heaven of divine wisdom is illumined with the two luminaries of consultation and compassion. Take ye counsel together in all matters, inasmuch as consultation is the lamp of guidance which leadeth the way, and is the bestower of understanding.

Bahá'u'lláh, *Consultation: A Compilation*, p. 3

February 12

In the East the light of His Revelation hath broken; in the West have appeared the signs of His dominion. Ponder this in your hearts, O people, and be not of those who have turned a deaf ear to the admonitions of Him Who is the Almighty, the All-Praised.   Bahá'u'lláh, *Citadel of Faith*, p. 30

"From the beginning of time until the present day the light of Divine Revelation hath risen in the East and shed its radiance upon the West. The illumination thus shed hath, however, acquired in the West an extraordinary brilliancy. Consider the Faith proclaimed by Jesus. Though it first appeared in the East, yet not until its light had been shed upon the West did the full measure of its potentialities become manifest." "The day is approaching when ye shall witness how, through the splendour of the Faith of Bahá'u'lláh the West will have replaced the East, radiating the light of divine guidance."

'Abdu'l-Bahá, *Citadel of Faith*, p. 30

February 13

O people of God! I admonish you to observe courtesy. For above all else it is the prince of virtues. Well is it with him who is illumined with the light of courtesy and is attired with the vesture of uprightness. Whoso is endued with courtesy hath indeed attained a sublime station. It is hoped that this Wronged One and everyone else may be enabled to acquire it, hold fast unto it, observe it, and fix our gaze upon it. This is a binding command which hath streamed forth from the Pen of the Most Great Name.   Bahá'u'lláh, *Tablets of Bahá'u'lláh*, p. 88

February 14

The vitality of men's belief in God is dying out in every land; nothing short of His wholesome medicine can ever restore it. The corrosion of ungodliness is eating into the vitals of human society; what else but the Elixir of His potent Revelation can cleanse and revive it? Is it within human power, O Hakím, to effect in the constituent elements of any of the minute and indivisible particles of matter so complete a transformation as to transmute it into purest gold? Perplexing and difficult as this may appear, the still greater task of converting satanic strength into heavenly power is one that We have been empowered to accomplish. . . . The Word of God, alone, can claim the distinction of being endowed with the capacity required for so great and far-reaching a change.

Bahá'u'lláh, *Gleanings from the Writings of Bahá'u'lláh*, p. 200

February 15

It is clear and evident that when the veils that conceal the realities of the manifestations of the Names and Attributes of God, nay of all created things visible or invisible, have been rent asunder, nothing except the Sign of God will remain—a sign which He, Himself, hath placed within these realities. This sign will endure as long as is the wish of the Lord thy God, the Lord of the heavens and of the earth. If such be the blessings conferred on all created things, how superior must be the destiny of the true believer, whose existence and life are to be regarded as the originating purpose of all creation. Just as the conception of faith hath existed from the beginning that hath no beginning, and will endure till the end that hath no end, in like manner will the true believer eternally live and endure. His spirit will everlastingly circle round the Will of God. He will last as long as God, Himself, will last. He is revealed through the Revelation of God, and is hidden at His bidding. It is evident that the loftiest mansions in the Realm of Immortality have been ordained as the habitation of them that have truly believed in God and in His signs. Death can never invade that holy seat. Thus have We entrusted thee with the signs of Thy Lord, that thou mayest persevere in thy love for Him, and be of them that comprehend this truth.

Bahá'u'lláh, *Gleanings from the Writings of Bahá'u'lláh*, pp. 140-141

February 16

O beloved of the Lord! If any soul speak ill of an absent one, the only result will clearly be this: he will dampen the zeal of the friends and tend to make them indifferent. For backbiting is divisive, it is the leading cause among the friends of a disposition to withdraw. If any individual should speak ill of one who is absent, it is incumbent on his hearers, in a spiritual and friendly manner, to stop him, and say in effect: would this detraction serve any useful purpose? Would it please the Blessed Beauty, contribute to the lasting honour of the friends, promote the holy Faith, support the Covenant, or be of any possible benefit to any soul? No, never! On the contrary, it would make the dust to settle so thickly on the heart that the ears would hear no more, and the eyes would no longer behold the light of truth.   'Abdu'l-Bahá, *Selections from the Writings of 'Abdu'l-Bahá*, pp. 230-231

February 17

In the next world man will find himself freed from many of the disabilities under which he now suffers. Those who have passed on through death, have a sphere of their own. It is not removed from ours: their work of the Kingdom, is ours; but it is sanctified from what we call time and place. Time with us is measured by the sun. When there is no more sunrise, and no more sunset, that kind of time does not exist for man. Those who have ascended have different attributes (conditions) from those who are still on earth, yet there is no real separation.

In prayer there is a mingling of stations, a mingling of condition. Pray for them as they pray for you.   'Abdu'l-Bahá, *The Divine Art of Living*, p. 124

February 18

To every discerning and illuminated heart it is evident that God, the unknowable Essence, the Divine Being, is immensely exalted beyond every human attribute, such as corporeal existence, ascent and descent, egress and regress. Far be it from His glory that human tongue should adequately recount His praise, or that human heart comprehend His fathomless mystery. He is, and hath ever been, veiled in the ancient eternity of His Essence, and will remain in His Reality everlastingly hidden from the sight of men. "No vision taketh in Him, but He taketh in all vision; He is the Subtile, the All-Perceiving." . . .

The door of the knowledge of the Ancient of Days being thus closed in the face of all beings, the

Source of infinite grace, according to His saying, "His grace hath transcended all things; My grace hath encompassed them all," hath caused those luminous Gems of Holiness to appear out of the realm of the spirit, in the noble form of the human temple, and be made manifest unto all men, that they may impart unto the world the mysteries of the unchangeable Being, and tell of the subtleties of His imperishable Essence.

Bahá'u'lláh, *Gleanings from the Writings of Bahá'u'lláh*, pp. 46-47

February 19

These sanctified Mirrors, these Day Springs of ancient glory, are, one and all, the Exponents on earth of Him Who is the central Orb of the universe, its Essence and ultimate Purpose. From Him proceed their knowledge and power; from Him is derived their sovereignty. The beauty of their countenance is but a reflection of His image, and their revelation a sign of His deathless glory. They are the Treasuries of Divine knowledge, and the Repositories of celestial wisdom. Through them is transmitted a grace that is infinite, and by them is revealed the Light that can never fade. . . . By the revelation of these Gems of Divine virtue all the names and attributes of God, such as knowledge and power, sovereignty and dominion, mercy and wisdom, glory, bounty, and grace, are made manifest.

These attributes of God are not, and have never been, vouchsafed specially unto certain Prophets, and withheld from others. Nay, all the Prophets of God, His well-favoured, His holy and chosen Messengers are, without exception, the bearers of His names, and the embodiments of His attributes. They only differ in the intensity of their revelation, and the comparative potency of their light.

Bahá'u'lláh, *Gleanings from the Writings of Bahá'u'lláh*, pp. 47-48

February 20

    . . . as man in the womb of the mother passes from form to form, from shape to shape, changes and develops, and is still the human species from the beginning of the embryonic period—in the same way man, from the beginning of his existence in the matrix of the world, is also a distinct species—that is, man—and has gradually evolved from one form to another. Therefore, this change of appearance, this evolution of members, this development and growth, even though we admit the reality of growth and progress, does not prevent the species from being original. Man from the beginning was in this perfect form and composition, and possessed capacity and aptitude for acquiring material and

spiritual perfections, and was the manifestation of
these words, "We will make man in Our image and
likeness". He has only become more pleasing, more
beautiful and more graceful. Civilization has
brought him out of his wild state, just as the wild
fruits which are cultivated by a gardener become
finer, sweeter and acquire more freshness and
delicacy.

The gardeners of the world of humanity are the
Prophets of God.

'Abdu'l-Bahá, *Some Answered Questions*,
(1982 edition) pp. 193-194

February 21

The wisdom of the appearance of the spirit in the body is this: the human spirit is a Divine Trust, and it must traverse all conditions, for its passage and movement through the conditions of existence will be the means of its acquiring perfections. So when a man travels and passes through different regions and numerous countries with system and method, it is certainly a means of his acquiring perfection, for he will see places, scenes and countries, from which he will discover the conditions and states of other nations. . . . It is the same when the human spirit passes through the conditions of existence: it will become the possessor of each degree and station. Even in the condition of the body it will surely acquire perfections.

'Abdu'l-Bahá, *Some Answered Questions*,
(1982 edition) pp. 200-201

February 22

Know that the Reality of Divinity or the substance of the Essence of Oneness is pure sanctity and absolute holiness—that is to say, it is sanctified and exempt from all praise. . . . It is invisible, incomprehensible, inaccessible, a pure essence which cannot be described . . .

Accordingly all these attributes, names, praises and eulogies apply to the Places of Manifestation [the Prophets of God]; and all that we imagine and suppose beside them is mere imagination, for we have no means of comprehending that which is invisible and inaccessible. . . . It is clear that if we wish to imagine the Reality of Divinity, this imagination is the surrounded, and we are the surrounding one; and it is sure that the one who surrounds is greater than the surrounded. . . .

Therefore, reflect that different peoples of the world are revolving around imaginations and are worshippers of the idols of thoughts and conjectures. They are not aware of this; they consider their imaginations to be the Reality which is withdrawn from all comprehension and purified from all descriptions. They regard themselves as the people of Unity, and the others as worshippers of idols; but idols at least have a mineral existence, while the idols of thoughts and the imaginations of man are but fancies; they have not even mineral existence.   'Abdu'l-Bahá, *Some Answered Questions*, (1981 edition) pp. 146-149

February 23

"The whole earth is now in a state of pregnancy. The day is approaching when it will have yielded its noblest fruits, when from it will have sprung forth the loftiest trees, the most enchanting blossoms, the most heavenly blessings. Immeasurably exalted is the breeze that wafteth from the garment of thy Lord, the Glorified! For lo, it hath breathed its fragrance and made all things new! Well is it with them that comprehend." "The onrushing winds of the grace of God have passed over all things. Every creature hath been endowed with all the potentialities it can carry. . . . The time is approaching when every created thing will have cast its burden. Glorified be God Who hath vouchsafed this grace that encompasseth all things, whether seen or unseen!"

Bahá'u'lláh, *The World Order of Bahá'u'lláh*, p. 169

February 24

Recall to mind My sorrows, My cares and anxieties, My woes and trials, the state of My captivity, the tears that I have shed, the bitterness of Mine anguish, and now Mine imprisonment in this far-off land . . . Couldst thou be told what hath befallen the Ancient Beauty, thou wouldst flee into the wilderness, and weep with a great weeping . . . Every morning I arose from my bed, I discovered the hosts of countless afflictions massed behind My door; and every night when I lay down, lo, My heart was torn with agony at what it had suffered from the fiendish cruelty of its foes.

Bahá'u'lláh, *The World Order of Bahá'u'lláh*, p. 174

February 25

Hence the unity of all mankind can in this day be achieved. Verily this is none other but one of the wonders of this wondrous age, this glorious century. Of this past ages have been deprived, for this century—the century of light—has been endowed with unique and unprecedented glory, power and illumination. . . .

Behold how its light is now dawning upon the world's darkened horizon. The first candle is unity in the political realm, the early glimmerings of which can now be discerned. The second candle is unity of thought in world undertakings, the consummation of which will ere long be witnessed. The third candle is unity in freedom which will surely come to pass. The fourth candle is unity in religion which is the corner-stone of the foundation itself, and which, by the power of God, will be revealed in all its splendour. The fifth candle is the unity of nations—a unity which in this century will be securely established, causing all the peoples of the world to regard themselves as citizens of one common fatherland. The sixth candle is unity of races, making all that dwell on earth peoples and kindreds of one race. The seventh candle is unity of language, i.e., the choice of a universal tongue in which all peoples will be instructed and converse. Each and every one of these will inevitably come to pass, inasmuch as the power of the Kingdom of God will aid and assist in their realization.

'Abdu'l-Bahá, *The World Order of Bahá'u'lláh*, p. 39

THE CELEBRATION OF AYYÁM-I-HÁ
——— BEGINS AT SUNSET ———

February 26

THE CELEBRATION OF AYYÁM-I-HÁ

We love to see you at all times consorting in amity and concord within the paradise of My good-pleasure, and to inhale from your acts the fragrance of friendliness and unity, of loving-kindness and fellowship. Thus counselleth you the All-Knowing, the Faithful. We shall always be with you; if We inhale the perfume of your fellowship, Our heart will assuredly rejoice, for naught else can satisfy Us. To this beareth witness every man of true understanding.   Bahá'u'lláh, *Gleanings from the Writings of Bahá'u'lláh*, pp. 315-316

February 27

THE CELEBRATION
OF AYYÁM-I-HÁ

Be ye sincerely kind, not in appearance only. Let each one of God's loved ones centre his attention on this: to be the Lord's mercy to man; to be the Lord's grace. Let him do some good to every person whose path he crosseth, and be of some benefit to him. Let him improve the character of each and all, and reorient the minds of men. In this way, the light of divine guidance will shine forth, and the blessings of God will cradle all mankind: for love is light, no matter in what abode it dwelleth; and hate is darkness, no matter where it may make its nest. O friends of God! That the hidden Mystery may stand revealed, and the secret essence of all things may be disclosed, strive ye to banish that darkness for ever and ever. 'Abdu'l-Bahá, *Selections from the Writings of 'Abdu'l-Bahá*, p. 3

February 28

THE CELEBRATION OF AYYÁM-I-HÁ

The utterance of God is a lamp, whose light are these words: Ye are the fruits of one tree, and the leaves of one branch. Deal ye one with another with the utmost love and harmony, with friendliness and fellowship. He Who is the Day-Star of Truth beareth Me witness! So powerful is the light of unity that it can illuminate the whole earth. The One true God, He Who knoweth all things, Himself testifieth to the truth of these words.

Bahá'u'lláh, Epistle to the Son of the Wolf, p. 14

February 29

THE CELEBRATION
OF AYYÁM-I-HÁ

Soon will your swiftly-passing days be over, and the fame and riches, the comforts, the joys provided by this rubbish-heap, the world, will be gone without a trace. Summon ye, then, the people to God, and invite humanity to follow the example of the Company on high. Be ye loving fathers to the orphan, and a refuge to the helpless, and a treasury for the poor, and a cure for the ailing. Be ye the helpers of every victim of oppression, the patrons of the disadvantaged. Think ye at all times of rendering some service to every member of the human race.

'Abdu'l-Bahá, *Selections from the Writings of 'Abdu'l-Bahá*, p. 3

March 1

THE CELEBRATION OF AYYÁM-I-HÁ

FEAST OF LOFTINESS

Fortunate are ye to have obeyed the commandment of God, and kept this fast during the holy season. For this material fast is an outer token of the spiritual fast; it is a symbol of self-restraint, the withholding of oneself from all appetites of the self, taking on the characteristics of the spirit, being carried away by the breathings of heaven and catching fire from the love of God.

Bahá'u'lláh, *Synopsis and Codification of the Kitab-i-Aqdas*, pp. 11-12

As regards fasting, it constitutes, together with the obligatory prayers, the two pillars that sustain the revealed Law of God. They act as stimulants to the soul, strengthen, revive, and purify it, and thus insure its steady development.

Shoghi Effendi, *Principles of Bahá'í Administration*, p. 8

THE MONTH OF LOFTINESS
THE MONTH OF FASTING—BEGINS AT SUNSET

March 2

THE FAST

O MY FRIENDS!
Have ye forgotten that true and radiant morn, when in those hallowed and blessed surroundings ye were all gathered in My presence beneath the shade of the tree of life, which is planted in the all-glorious paradise? Awe-struck ye listened as I gave utterance to these three most holy words: O friends! Prefer not your will to Mine, never desire that which I have not desired for you, and approach Me not with lifeless hearts, defiled with worldly desires and cravings. Would ye but sanctify your souls, ye would at this present hour recall that place and those surroundings, and the truth of My utterance should be made evident unto all of you.

Bahá'u'lláh, *The Hidden Words of Bahá'u'lláh*,
No. 19 (Persian)

March 3

THE FAST

In the Prayer of Fasting We have revealed: "Should Thy Will decree that out of Thy mouth these words proceed and be addressed unto them, 'Observe, for My Beauty's sake, the fast, O people, and set no limit to its duration,' I swear by the majesty of Thy glory, that every one of them will faithfully observe it, will abstain from whatsoever will violate Thy law, and will continue to do so until they yield up their souls unto Thee." In this consisteth the complete surrender of one's will to the Will of God. Meditate on this, that thou mayest drink in the waters of everlasting life which flow through the words of the Lord of all mankind, and mayest testify that the one true God hath ever been immeasurably exalted above His creatures. . . .
The station of absolute self-surrender transcendeth, and will ever remain exalted above, every other station.

Bahá'u'lláh, *Gleanings from the Writing of Bahá'u'lláh*, pp. 337-338

March 4

THE FAST

. . . O thou who hast surrendered thy will to God! By self-surrender and perpetual union with God is meant that men should merge their will wholly in the Will of God, and regard their desires as utter nothingness beside His Purpose. Whatsoever the Creator commandeth His creatures to observe, the same must they diligently, and with the utmost joy and eagerness, arise and fulfil. They should in no wise allow their fancy to obscure their judgment, neither should they regard their own imaginings as the voice of the Eternal.

Bahá'u'lláh, *Gleanings from the Writings of Bahá'u'lláh*, p. 337

March 5

THE FAST

O My brother! When a true seeker determineth
to take the step of search in the path leading unto the
knowledge of the Ancient of Days, he must, before
all else, cleanse his heart, which is the seat of the
revelation of the inner mysteries of God, from the
obscuring dust of all acquired knowledge, and the
allusions of the embodiments of satanic fancy. He
must purge his breast, which is the sanctuary of the
abiding love of the Beloved, of every defilement,
and sanctify his soul from all that pertaineth to water
and clay, from all shadowy and ephemeral
attachments. He must so cleanse his heart that no
remnant of either love or hate may linger therein,
lest that love blindly incline him to error, or that hate
repel him away from the truth.

Bahá'u'lláh, *Gleanings from the Writings
of Bahá'u'lláh*, p. 264

March 6

THE FAST

That seeker must, at all times, put his trust in God, must renounce the peoples of the earth, must detach himself from the world of dust, and cleave unto Him Who is the Lord of Lords. He must never seek to exalt himself above any one, must wash away from the tablet of his heart every trace of pride and vain-glory, must cling unto patience and resignation, observe silence and refrain from idle talk. For the tongue is a smoldering fire, and excess of speech a deadly poison. Material fire consumeth the body, whereas the fire of the tongue devoureth both heart and soul. The force of the former lasteth but for a time, whilst the effects of the latter endureth a century.

Bahá'u'lláh, *Gleanings from the Writings of Bahá'u'lláh*, pp. 264-265

March 7

THE FAST

That seeker should, also, regard backbiting as grievous error, and keep himself aloof from its dominion, inasmuch as backbiting quencheth the light of the heart, and extinguisheth the life of the soul. . . . He should not wish for others that which he doth not wish for himself, nor promise that which he doth not fulfil. With all his heart he should avoid fellowship with evil-doers, and pray for the remission of their sins. He should forgive the sinful, and never despise his low estate, for none knoweth what his own end shall be. How often hath a sinner attained, at the hour of death, to the essence of faith, and, quaffing the immortal draught, hath taken his flight unto the Concourse on high! And how often hath a devout believer, at the hour of his soul's ascension, been so changed as to fall into the nethermost fire! Bahá'u'lláh, *Gleanings form the Writings of Bahá'u'lláh*, pp. 265-266

March 8

THE FAST

Only when the lamp of search, of earnest striving, of longing desire, of passionate devotion, of fervid love, of rapture, and ecstasy, is kindled within the seeker's heart, and the breeze of His loving-kindness is wafted upon his soul, will the darkness of error be dispelled, the mists of doubts and misgivings be dissipated, and the lights of knowledge and certitude envelop his being. . . . Then will the manifold favours and outpouring grace of the holy and everlasting Spirit confer such new life upon the seeker that he will find himself endowed with a new eye, a new ear, a new heart, and a new mind. Gazing with the eye of God, he will perceive within every atom a door that leadeth him to the stations of absolute certitude. He will discover in all things the mysteries of Divine Revelation, and the evidences of an everlasting Manifestation.

Bahá'u'lláh, *Gleanings from the Writings of Bahá'u'lláh*, p. 267

March 9

When the channel of the human soul is cleansed of all worldly and impeding attachments, it will unfailingly perceive the breath of the Beloved across immeasurable distances, and will, led by its perfume, attain and enter the City of Certitude. . . .

That City is none other than the Word of God revealed in every age and dispensation. In the days of Moses it was the Pentateuch; in the days of Jesus, the Gospel; in the days of Muhammad, the Messenger of God, the Qur'an; in this day, the Bayan; and in the Dispensation of Him Whom God will make manifest, His own Book—the Book unto which all the Books of former Dispensations must needs be referred, the Book that standeth amongst them all transcendent and supreme.

Bahá'u'lláh, *Gleanings from the Writings of Bahá'u'lláh*, p. 267-269

March 10

THE FAST

Far, far from Thy glory be what mortal man can affirm of Thee, or attribute unto Thee, or the praise with which he can glorify Thee! Whatever duty Thou hast prescribed unto Thy servants of extolling to the utmost Thy majesty and glory is but a token of Thy grace unto them, that they may be enabled to ascend unto the station conferred upon their own inmost being, the station of the knowledge of their own selves.

No one else besides Thee hath, at any time, been able to fathom Thy mystery, or befittingly to extol Thy greatness. Unsearchable and high above the praise of men wilt Thou remain for ever. There is none other God but Thee, the Inaccessible, the Omnipotent, the Omniscient, the Holy of Holies.

Bahá'u'lláh, *Gleanings from the Writings of Bahá'u'lláh*, pp. 4-5

March 11

THE FAST

O ye peoples of the world! Know assuredly that My commandments are the lamps of My loving providence among My servants, and the keys of My mercy for My creatures. Thus hath it been sent down from the heaven of the Will of your Lord, the Lord of Revelation. Were any man to taste the sweetness of the words which the lips of the All-Merciful have willed to utter, he would, though the treasures of the earth be in his possession, renounce them one and all, that he might vindicate the truth of even one of His commandments, shining above the Dayspring of His bountiful care and loving-kindness.

Bahá'u'lláh, *Synopsis and Codification of the Kitáb-i-Aqdas*, p. 12

March 12

THE FAST

Say: If ye be seekers after this life and the vanities thereof, ye should have sought them while ye were still enclosed in your mothers' wombs, for at that time ye were continually approaching them, could ye but perceive it. Ye have, on the other hand, ever since ye were born and attained maturity, been all the while receding from the world and drawing closer to dust. Why, then, exhibit such greed in amassing the treasures of the earth, when your days are numbered and your chance is well-nigh lost? Will ye not, then, O heedless ones, shake off your slumber?

Incline your ears to the counsels which this Servant giveth you for the sake of God. He, verily, asketh no recompense from you and is resigned to what God hath ordained for Him, and is entirely submissive to God's Will.

Bahá'u'lláh, *Gleanings from the Writings of Bahá'u'lláh*, p. 127

March 13

THE FAST

The days of your life are far spent, O people, and your end is fast approaching. Put away, therefore, the things ye have devised and to which ye cleave, and take firm hold on the precepts of God, that haply ye may attain that which He hath purposed for you, and be of them that pursue a right course. Delight not yourselves in the things of the world and its vain ornaments, neither set your hopes on them. Let your reliance be on the remembrance of God, the Most Exalted, the Most Great. He will, ere long, bring to naught all the things ye possess. Let Him be your fear, and forget not His covenant with you, and be not of them that are shut out as by a veil from Him. Bahá'u'lláh, *Gleanings from the Writings of Bahá'u'lláh*, pp. 127-128

March 14

THE FAST

Beware that ye swell not with pride before God, and disdainfully reject His loved ones. Defer ye humbly to the faithful, they that have believed in God and in His signs, whose hearts witness to His unity, whose tongues proclaim His oneness, and who speak not except by His leave. Thus do We exhort you with justice, and warn you with truth, that perchance ye may be awakened.

Lay not on any soul a load which ye would not wish to be laid upon you, and desire not for any one the things ye would not desire for yourselves. This is My best counsel unto you, did ye but observe it.

Bahá'u'lláh, *Gleanings from the Writings
of Bahá'u'lláh*, p. 128

March 15

THE FAST

Know ye that trials and tribulations have, from time immemorial, been the lot of the chosen Ones of God and His beloved, and such of His servants as are detached from all else but Him, . . . Such is God's method carried into effect of old, and such will it remain in the future. Blessed are the steadfastly enduring, they that are patient under ills and hardships, who lament not over anything that befalleth them, and who tread the path of resignation.

Bahá'u'lláh, *Gleanings from the Writings of Bahá'u'lláh*, p. 129

March 16

THE FAST

The day is approaching when God will have raised up a people who will call to remembrance Our days, who will tell the tale of Our trials, who will demand the restitution of Our rights from them that, without a tittle of evidence, have treated Us with manifest injustice. God, assuredly, dominateth the lives of them that wronged Us, and is well aware of their doings. He will, most certainly, lay hold on them for their sins. He, verily, is the fiercest of avengers. Bahá'u'lláh, *Gleanings from the Writings of Bahá'u'lláh*, pp. 129-130

March 17

THE FAST

Thus have We recounted unto you the tales of the one true God, and sent down unto you the things He had preordained, that haply ye may ask forgiveness of Him, may return unto Him, may truly repent, may realize your misdeeds, may shake off your slumber, may be roused from your heedlessness, may atone for the things that have escaped you, and be of them that do good. . . . Wherefore, hearken ye unto My speech, and return ye to God and repent, that He, through His grace, may have mercy upon you, may wash away your sins, and forgive your trespasses. The greatness of His mercy surpasseth the fury of His wrath, and His grace encompasseth all who have been called into being and been clothed with the robe of life, be they of the past or of the future.

Bahá'u'lláh, *Gleanings from the Writings of Bahá'u'lláh*, p. 130

March 18

THE FAST

"Great mercy and blessings are promised to the people of your land [North America], but on one condition: that their hearts are filled with the fire of love, that they live in perfect kindness and harmony like one soul in different bodies. If they fail in this condition the great blessings will be deferred. Never forget this; look at one another with the eye of perfection; look at Me, follow Me, be as I am; take no thought for yourselves or your lives, whether ye eat or whether ye sleep, whether ye are comfortable, whether ye are well or ill, whether ye are with friends or foes, whether ye receive praise or blame; for all of these things ye must care not at all. Look at Me and be as I am; ye must die to yourselves and to the world, so shall ye be born again and enter the Kingdom of Heaven. Behold a candle how it gives its light. It weeps its life away drop by drop in order to give forth its flame of light.

'Abdu'l-Bahá, *An Early Pilgrimage*, pp. 41-42

March 19

THE FAST

O Brother! Not every sea hath pearls; not every branch will flower, nor will the nightingale sing thereon. Then, ere the nightingale of the mystic paradise repair to the garden of God, and the rays of the heavenly morning return to the Sun of Truth—make thou an effort, that haply in this dustheap of the mortal world thou mayest catch a fragrance from the everlasting garden, and live forever in the shadow of the peoples of this city. And when thou hast attained this highest station and come to this mightiest plane, then shalt thou gaze on the Beloved, and forget all else.

Bahá'u'lláh, *The Seven Valleys and the Four Valleys*, p. 38

March 20

THE FAST

The mystic and wondrous Bride, hidden ere this beneath the veiling of utterance, hath now, by the grace of God and His divine favour, been made manifest even as the resplendent light shed by the beauty of the Beloved. I bear witness, O friends! that the favour is complete, the argument fulfilled, the proof manifest and the evidence established. Let it now be seen what your endeavours in the path of detachment will reveal. In this wise hath the divine favour been fully vouchsafed unto you and unto them that are in heaven and on earth. All praise to God, the Lord of all Worlds.

Bahá'u'lláh, *The Hidden Words of Bahá'u'lláh*, pp. 51-52

THE CELEBRATION OF NAW-RÚZ,
THE MONTH OF SPLENDOUR,
AND THE NEW BAHÁ'Í YEAR
ALL BEGIN AT SUNSET

THE REVELATION OF
BAHÁ'U'LLÁH

The Revelation of Bahá'u'lláh, whose supreme mission is none other but the achievement of this organic and spiritual unity of the whole body of nations, should, if we be faithful to its implications, be regarded as signalizing through its advent the coming of age of the entire human race. It should be viewed not merely as yet another spiritual revival in the ever-changing fortunes of mankind, not only as a further stage in a chain of progressive Revelations, nor even as the culmination of one of a series of recurrent prophetic cycles, but rather as marking the last and highest stage in the stupendous evolution of man's collective life on this planet. The emergence of a world community, the consciousness of world citizenship, the founding of a world civilization and culture—all of which must synchronize with the initial stages and the unfoldment of the Golden Age of the Bahá'í Era—should, by their very nature, be regarded, as far as this planetary life is concerned, as the furthermost limits in the organization of human

society, though man, as an individual, will, nay
must indeed as a result of such a consummation,
continue indefinitely to progress and develop.

Shoghi Effendi, *The World Order of Bahá'u'lláh*, p. 163

THE NATURE OF
DEEPENING

The beloved Guardian wrote, "To strive to
obtain a more adequate understanding of the
significance of Bahá'u'lláh's stupendous Revelation must, it is my unalterable conviction, remain
the first obligation and the object of the constant
endeavour of each one of its loyal adherents," a
statement which places the obligation of deepening
in the Cause firmly on every believer. It is therefore
upon the nature of deepening, rather than upon the
desirability of pursuing it, that we wish to comment.

A detailed and exact knowledge of the present
structure of Bahá'í administration, or of the bylaws
of national and local spiritual assemblies, or of the
many and varied applications of Bahá'í law under
the diverse conditions prevailing around the world,

while valuable in itself, cannot be regarded as the sort of knowledge primarily intended by deepening. Rather is suggested a clearer apprehension of the purpose of God for man, and particularly of His immediate purpose as revealed and directed by Bahá'u'lláh, a purpose as far removed from current concepts of human well-being and happiness as is possible. . . . Referring to the ". . . epoch-making changes that constitute the greatest landmarks in the history of human civilization," he states that ". . . they cannot appear, when viewed in their proper perspective, except as subsidiary adjustments preluding that transformation of unparalleled majesty and scope which humanity is in this age bound to undergo." In a later document he refers to the civilization to be established by Bahá'u'lláh as one ". . . with a fullness of life such as the world has never seen nor can as yet conceive."

Dearly-loved friends, this is the theme we must pursue in our efforts to deepen in the Cause. What is Bahá'u'lláh's purpose for the human race? For what ends did He submit to the appalling cruelties and indignities heaped upon Him? What does He mean by "a new race of men"? What are the profound

389

changes which He will bring about? The answers are to be found in the Sacred Writings of our Faith and in their interpretation by 'Abdu'l-Bahá and our beloved Guardian. Let the friends immerse themselves in this ocean, let them organize regular study classes for its constant consideration, and, as reinforcement to their effort, let them remember conscientiously the requirements of daily prayer and reading of the Word of God enjoined upon all Bahá'ís by Bahá'u'lláh.

Universal House of Justice, *Wellspring of Guidance*, pp. 113-115

March 19 "Not every sea hath pearls..."

August 21
LOVE
"Know thou .. that love is the secret....."

Jan. 14
FAITH
"... I will be with you till the end

July 28th • Gods love for me
this, empathy,
June 24th • Death / Fear
June 5 Clay of Love

Sept. 19 Love is light
Help each person

July 12 Meetings!

July 16 Consultation

Feb. 10 meditation, silence,
intellect,
June 27th Investigating Truth

Publications
BaháʼíCanada
Publications

7200 Leslie Street
Thornhill, Ontario L3T 2Al

Printed in Canada

July 26 possession